Praise for
Living Rich for Less

"Ellie Kay makes complicated financial concepts understandable. Heeding her advice will give you an extraordinary quality of life as you learn the secrets of living and giving in a way that multiplies your resources."

>—CAROL KENT, best-selling author *A New Kind of Normal*
>and president of Speak Up Speaker Services

"We feel richer already! Ellie Kay gives a billfold full of ideas to help place more money back into your pockets! With three kids in college and retirement on the horizon, Ellie's wisdom is a wealth of encouragement, comfort, and practical proven helps."

>—PAM AND BILL FARREL, international speakers, best-selling
>authors of *Men Are like Waffles, Women Are like Spaghetti,*
>and *Ten Best Decisions a Couple Can Make*

Praise for Ellie Kay

"Ellie's work, helping us be better stewards, is one of the great services to families across our nation."

>—DENNIS RAINEY, executive director and radio host of FamilyLife

"Ellie is amazing! I don't think she ever sleeps! She provides great information and is always a fun guest on the show."

>—BILL GRIFFITH, host of CNBC's *Power Lunch*

"Ellie is the gateway to mainstream America."

>—MARC MYERS, money columnist, *Reader's Digest*

"A splendid example of the far-reaching and positive impact that an individual with vision and faith can make in our world. Thank God for people like her who are a tremendous inspiration!"

—DR. ROBERT H. SCHULLER, The Crystal Cathedral
and television host of *Hour of Power*

"Ellie provides an amazing abundance of helpful and insightful information."

—DR. NORM WRIGHT, best-selling author and licensed marriage,
child, and family therapist

"She makes things simple so even I can understand it."

—DR. KEVIN LEMAN, best-selling author of *Making Your Children
Mind Without Losing Yours* and *Have a New Kid By Friday*

"The debt mentality in our society is rampant, and people are desperate. Ellie hits the nail on the head by defining those struggles and offering practical solutions in a remarkably clear way."

—HOWARD DAYTON, CEO, Crown Financial Ministries

"A gifted communicator…interesting, educational, and very helpful. I recommend her work wholeheartedly to any family in America."

—RON BLUE, president CFP Network

"Provides the world's most practical information on family finances. She gives real answers for real people dealing with real finances in a real world."

—PHIL WALDREP, author of *Parenting Prodigals*

LIVING
RICH
for
LESS

HOW YOU
CAN SAVE
$30,000
THIS YEAR

Also by Ellie Kay

A Mom's Guide to Family Finances
A Woman's Guide to Family Finances
A Tip a Day with Ellie Kay
Half-Price Living
Heroes at Home
How to Save Money Every Day
Kisses of Sunshine for Moms
Money Doesn't Grow on Trees
Shop, Save, and Share
The Debt Diet
The New Bride Guide

The Cha Ching Factor™ Index

How You Can Save $30,000+ This Year

In 2008, housing resale sunk to a twenty-three-year low, and more people lost homes than in the previous decade. Follow the Cha Ching tip in the introduction to keep from foreclosure or loss of equity: Save at least $20,000.

Use the 10/10/90 Debt Rule chart in the introduction to offset accumulated consumer debt over fifteen years: Save $72,562.

For each vehicle purchased, use the 10/10/90 Debt Rule on devaluation and interest rates: Save between $5,000 and $8,000.

For every $2,500 in taxes overwithheld: Earn approximately $150 in interest equity.

File taxes as married jointly, making $65,000 a year and tithing $6,500 (in the 25 percent tax bracket) to itemize a minimum deduction: Benefit of $1,625 in estimated tax savings.

Prevent an unqualified removal of $10,000 from a 401(k) or IRA, which the introduction explains costs in penalties, interest, and tax: Save $1,050.

Invest a 401(k) in mutual funds, and claim the matching benefit that many companies offer—as the Kay family did (at 100 percent up to $5,000): Earn $5,000 per year.

Refinance a $200,000 home at an interest rate 1.5 percent lower than the existing loan and with minimal closing costs (assuming a twelve-month period on recovery costs): Save $22,123 over the course of a thirty-year loan, or $737 per year.

Donate a total of $800 in items to Goodwill, as Heather's family in chapter 2: Save $224 on taxes.

Through the church pantry, donate $445 a year, as Stephen's family did in chapter 2: Benefit of $111 in tax savings.

Use Ellie Kay's cost-savings tips as Kelli from New Mexico did to afford health insurance at $600: Save $44,000 on a $45,000 medical bill.

Buy and use a CFL for every light bulb in your house (nine bulbs on average): Save $270 over the life of the bulb.

The Consumer Expenditure Survey indicates that energy costs have risen 16.6 percent, causing the average American family to pay more than $3,600 per year in utilities. Follow the tips in chapter 3: Reduce what you pay on utilities by 15 percent and save $540.

Invest one dollar a day for ten years at 10 percent interest (as in the chart in chapter 4): Yield $6,145.

Use the dual-enrollment options explained in chapter 4 for a two-year associate's degree: Save $3,200 at in-state tuition rates.

Most consumers get six late fees per year on a variety of bills at an average penalty of $30 each. Use chapter 5's tips to pay on time: Save $180.

Mind your limits on credit and checking accounts, unlike the average consumer who exceeds their limits twice a year: Save $56.

Avoid a $100 cash advance three times a year: Save an average of $45.

Ask two of your credit card companies if you can avoid paying the annual fee for being a good customer: Save $40 per card or $80.

Order each of your three credit reports for free instead of paying for them: Save $60.

Read the fine print to avoid a 3 percent balance transfer fee on total transfer amounts of $3,000: Save $90.

Forgo traveler's checks, which cost an average of $1 per $100 (most travelers buy $1,500 worth): Save $15 on fees and an average of ten cents on the dollar for credit card exchange rates (versus cash) and savings on fee services for currency exchange. This is a savings of $300 on $3,000 worth of hotel fees, rentals, gifts, tickets, etc. The two save a total of $315.

Take a card with a 1 percent fee rather than 3 percent for $3,000 worth of overseas transactions: Save $60.

Refinance your home and drop your mortgage rate (from 9.28 to 5.48 percent), following the steps in chapter 6 to help improve your FICO score (from 599 to 720): Save $4,644 per year as payments go from $1,238 to $851 a month.

On your homeowner's insurance, as in chapter 8, be sure to insure the value of the house itself and not the dirt it's on: Save approximately $250 per year.

On auto insurance, take every discount possible—for the average two-car family with a youthful driver, for example, combine a homeowner's and auto policy, be a nonsmoker and good student, install a car alarm system, store the vehicle in a garage versus carport or on the street, and ask how your policy is rated (a stay-at-home mom's vehicle or one for pleasure is less expensive to insure, and discounts exist for drivers with a safety course certificate): Save $900 per year.

On vacation, rent an RV and cook in versus staying at a hotel and eating out: Save an average of $500 per week per family, or $1,000 for two annual vacations.

Follow the online tips in chapter 10 for finding the lowest price on items you need with a shopping robot at mySimon.com or Froogle.com, use a code site to get free shipping or postage and handling and other discounts at Dealhunting.com or CouponCabin.com, or get rebates at Ebates.com: Save $1,200 per year.

Learn to negotiate like an Apprentice in chapter 9: Save $1,800 per year on the topics covered.

Buy and use the coupons in a $25 to $45 Entertainment.com coupon book for 150 metropolitan markets, as in chapter 9: Save $17,000 on dining out, movie tickets, theme park entrance fees, dry cleaning, and local shopping.

Redeem just 25 percent of the coupons in an entertainment discount book: Save $4,250 per year.

Use coupons and gift certificates from Restaurant.com—good for more than 6,000 eateries around the country: Save 30 to 50 percent on bills eating out. (In one example, the Kay family picks a spot, pays $25 for a $50 gift certificate, and saves 50 percent in the process. The average restaurant bill for a family of four is $86, so that family can save $43 a week or $2,236 per year.)

Follow the insider tips in chapter 10 for a $199 per person cruise (plus additional services and excursions): Save $2,500 per couple.

Through the detailed tips on a "family meeting," learn how to get everyone to buy into a family vacation: Save 20 percent, or a total $750 from the average $2,500 vacation.

Double up with friends or family on vacation, as the typical family of four in chapter 10: Cut bills in half, saving $1,250 in rental fees and $2,500 in general expenses (even more if you share the cooking chores and eat in).

Update or redecorate your home with a $65 to $100 quality slipcover instead of buying a new sofa for $850. Place a $15 linen runner or crocheted doily on a table scratched by a speeding Corvette, Hot Wheels size, instead of buying a new coffee table for $130. Repair broken tiles and chipped grout around sinks or tubs to minimize water damage ($30) rather than having to retile at a cost of $350: Save a total $1,185 room by room.

Check out page 163 on fuel costs; make sure the air pressure in your tires is proper, take the junk from the trunk, change your air filters frequently, and drive 65 miles per hour where it's posted 70: Save 25 percent, or $750, in fuel efficiency per car this next year.

The next time you clothes shop, look for clearance sales. Ask the salesclerks to check the back for your size (not all clearance items are always out front), and learn how to ask a clerk to check another store, give you the sale price, and ship the item for free (more stores offer this service to compete with online retailers). Like Ellie, purchase six pairs of jeans for the kids with original prices of $60 and sale prices of $20: Save $240.

Layer savings on food shopping like the average family of four, which the USDA reports spends $7,968 per year, by combining store sales, coupons, double coupons, "cash off your next shopping trip," and in-store coupons: Save $3,900 per year.

Instead of dinner and a movie ($80 a night), follow the tips on page 198 for fifty-two free weekly date nights per year with the one you love: Save $4,160 annually.

Maintain a home with the tips in chapter 11 (on everything from regular termite inspections to energy loss): Save $97,200 by avoiding home neglect and ruin.

LIVING RICH for LESS

HOW YOU
CAN SAVE
$30,000
THIS YEAR

Create the Lifestyle You Want *by*
Giving, Saving, *and* Spending Smart

ELLIE KAY

America's Family Financial Expert®

WATERBROOK
PRESS

LIVING RICH FOR LESS
PUBLISHED BY WATERBROOK PRESS
12265 Oracle Boulevard, Suite 200
Colorado Springs, Colorado 80921

Details in some anecdotes and stories have been changed to protect the identities of the persons involved.

ISBN 978-0-30744-601-5
ISBN 978-0-30744-602-2 (electronic)

Copyright © 2008 by Ellie Kay

The 10/10/80 Rule™, the Cha Ching Factor™, and the Living R.I.C.H.™ Principle are trademarks of Ellie Kay & Company, LLC.

All rights reserved. No part of this book may be reproduced or transmitted in any form or by any means, electronic or mechanical, including photocopying and recording, or by any information storage and retrieval system, without permission in writing from the publisher.

Published in the United States by WaterBrook Multnomah, an imprint of The Doubleday Publishing Group, a division of Random House Inc., New York.

WATERBROOK and its deer colophon are registered trademarks of Random House Inc.

Library of Congress Cataloging-in-Publication Data
Kay, Ellie.
   Living rich for less : create the lifestyle you want by giving, saving, and spending smart / Ellie Kay.
      p. cm.
   ISBN 978-0-30744-601-5
   1. Finance, Personal. 2. Saving and investment. 3. Consumer education. 4. Lifestyles—Economic aspects. I. Title.
   HG179.K3789 2008
   332.024—dc22

                              2008041570

Printed in the United States of America
2008—First Edition

10 9 8 7 6 5 4 3 2 1

SPECIAL SALES
Most WaterBrook Multnomah books are available in special quantity discounts when purchased in bulk by corporations, organizations, and special-interest groups. Custom imprinting or excerpting can also be done to fit special needs. For information, please e-mail SpecialMarkets@WaterBrook Multnomah.com or call 1-800-603-7051.

To the One who would rather die than live without me.

Contents

Introduction

Mr. and Ms. America: *The New Superheroes: Savers, Spenders,*
and Givers 1

Part 1

Giving 10 Percent:

The sweetest dollar you ever make is the one you give away 17

1 Little Miss Giver: *Giving It Away Will Make You Rich* 19
2 Little Moneybags Grows Up: *Four Ways to Give like*
   a Child 37
3 Giving Green: *Eco-Friendly Savings for Energy, the*
   Environment, and Eggplant 63

Part 2

Saving 10 Percent:

The safest dollar you ever make is the one you put away 77

4 Investing for Idiots: *Forrest Funds a Dream* 81
5 Fat Tuesday: *The Debt Debate* 107
6 Fun, Fun, Fun!: *The FICO Factor* 131
7 The 10/10/80 Budget for "Special" People: *How to*
   Develop a Workable Plan 147

Part 3

Spending Smart the Other 80 Percent:

The smartest dollar you ever make is the one you spend well 155

8   The New Cool: *Slashing Insurance Costs, and Room-by-Room Cash Savings* 159

9   Shopping to Save: *Shop-Till-You-Drop Savings on Groceries, on Clothing, and Online* 175

10   Cruisin' to Vacation Savings: *Travel, Entertain, and Eat Out Affordably* 187

11   Bubble, Bubble, Toil, and Trouble: *Attain and Maintain the Home of Your Dreams* 201

12   The 10/10/80 Legacy: *Living Rich in the Ways That Matter Most* 215

Acknowledgments 221

Notes 223

Introduction

Mr. and Ms. America

The New Superheroes: Savers, Spenders, and Givers

Batman, Wonder Woman, Spider-Man, and X-Men all have something more in common than being comic book characters. They are part of a dream, the American Dream, the dream each of us wants, whether we admit it or not. Wonder Woman, for example, is drop-dead gorgeous, and her 38-inch inseam makes me want to get leg extension surgery; if my husband had Wolverine's abs, I'd be a lot more patient when he missed yet another highway exit because he's fiddling with the satellite radio. Again. And if any of my kids had Bruce Wayne's wealth? I might never have to clip another coupon in my life!

I may not be a superhero, but I've learned how to do practically supernatural things with money—like help people save $30,000 in the next year.

How can I make such a claim?

Because I've been there and done that. My family tried for years to get ahead, even before these taxed-out, maxed-out times, and we found the tried-and-true way to live rich. The really cool thing is that I believe there's a superhero embedded in you—one waiting to make a grand entrance and save America from financial disaster. For every family that becomes financially solid, we build a firmer economic foundation for our country.

Therefore, you can save America by saving yourself and unleashing your inner superhero!

I'll call you "Mr. and Ms. America."

This book is for you, written by someone (and her family) who was average by day but ambitious by night, dreaming of

- getting out of debt.
- owning our cars outright.
- buying a dream house.
- putting our kids through college debt free.
- learning the ins and outs of saving and investing cash.

The thing is, I didn't stop with a dream. That's where it began. Then there was a process, and now, on an average American salary, we've seen all those dreams come true. We've discovered that there is a rich lifestyle embedded in our checkbook. There's one in yours too, and I'll help you discover it so you can make a life and not just a living.

My greatest ambition is to help Mr. and Ms. America live rich for less.

If you're wondering whether you're the Mr. and Ms. America who can find similar financial success, realize that the average family makes $48,000 per year, and an amazing 85 percent of the population makes $100,000 or less. I'll leave the top 15 percent of the nation's wealthiest to experts like Jim Cramer and Suze Orman. I'd rather help people who come from an average background to find above-average success. People like us.

When I first met Bob, my husband, I was searching for my own personal Superman. If he looked like Christopher Reeve, all the better! I never expected him to fly in on a jet. But alas, my superhero really was a pilot named K-Bob, and I found that time flew around this guy as well. I protested, "When I'm with you, time goes by so quickly that if I married you, I'd be an old lady before I knew it!"

I gave in and married the flyboy, just yesterday...or so it seems. I left my job as a broker and followed my guy around the world. Today we're living the rich life, but it wasn't always that way. Our early marriage was filled with major villains, like the Joker of debt and the Lex Luthor of near bankruptcy.

When I married the guy in tight tights, I found myself with a three-for-one deal, because not only did I get a great guy, but I also inherited two beautiful stepdaughters in the process. As with many second families, we struggled with the financial aftermath of divorce, which included $40,000 of consumer debt with nothing to show for it. In those early years, a cross-stitch sampler on our wall summed up our situation well: "Blessed are the poor, for they be us." We had trouble making ends meet and even struggled with the ability to pay the rent and buy groceries.

Here's what our portfolio of bills looked like:

- **Uncle Sam**—one-third of Bob's income went to taxes.
- **Child Support**—another third went to child support, and medical insurance, and more for Bob's two daughters.
- **Charitable Giving**—we tithed 10 percent off the top.
- **Living Expenses**—we lived on the other 23 percent and also serviced our $40,000 in debt with this portion.

We did the math and discovered that we were essentially living on the equivalent of an airman (one of the lowest enlisted ranks in the air force) even though Bob was a captain and a pilot. Then the situation became even more complicated.

Our family grew, and we had a total of five children in seven years. As a blended family, we now had seven children to support. Bob's military career included eleven moves in the first thirteen years of our marriage. It became plain, very early on, that it would be impractical for me to go back to being an insurance broker.

Nonetheless, I didn't regret staying home with our children. I rolled up my shirtsleeves, took my business education and experience, and channeled my energy and know-how into paying down debt and learning to save money.

Two and a half years later, we were completely debt free and have remained free of consumer debt ever since.

That's rich!

But then it got even better.

On a military man's salary, with me as a SAHM (stay-at-home mom), we were able to recover financially and in fifteen years pay cash for eleven different cars, give away three of those cars, buy two five-bedroom homes (one after selling the other), take regular family vacations, nicely furnish our home, clothe our kids in style, and support more than thirty nonprofit organizations in a dozen different countries by giving away more than $100,000.

Today our kids are on track to graduate from college debt free, and we have a nice nest egg for retirement with a home that by then will be paid for with no debt. We also have a fully funded 401(k), an SEP, Roth IRAs, mutual funds, and other investments.

Living in a nice home, paying the bills, driving paid-for cars, putting your kids through college, and having money for retirement—isn't *that* the rich life?

Attain and Maintain

To me, being rich is the idea of finding security in a world that can never really be secure. After those early years of struggling to find the money to buy groceries and diapers, I shouted like Scarlett O'Hara in *Gone with the Wind* that I never wanted to be hungry again, neither me nor any of my kin. I wanted to have the choice of shopping at a garage sale or a mall, but in those early years there was no choice. I wanted a safety net in a world that was unsafe. Living rich meant living well and living without worry. It also meant finding that supernatural balance between needs and wants and between contentment and desire. In the process, I found myself to be a former ragamuffin, Eliza Doolittle, who became *My Fair Lady*, when I discovered the timeless financial truths and exclaimed, "I think I've got it!"

What I discovered were the specific steps someone (that means you!) can take to attain the lifestyle you want, the lifestyle that allows you to maintain a quality of life that's important to you. Bob and I learned a lot during the first couple years of marriage, and our solution wasn't just a quick fix—it was a long-term plan.

This book will show you, step by step, how to find that $30,000-plus in the next year and how to attain and maintain a rich lifestyle by practicing the 10/10/80 Rule™, the Cha Ching Factor™, and the Living R.I.C.H.™ Principle.

- The philosophical marries the practical in the 10/10/80 Rule because there has to be a reason behind the way we earn, save, and spend our financial resources. This rule serves as a guide for the how-to part of gaining wealth.
- The Cha Ching Factor is just plain fun, as you will learn throughout this book the dollar amounts you can save during the year.
- The Living R.I.C.H. Principle demonstrates the mind-set and actions needed to become debt free and live that way.

Thanks for joining me on this lifestyle of rich living. The degree of success you experience depends entirely upon you, but I know you can make wise choices that will benefit you, your family, and even your worldwide community. Together we'll watch you create the lifestyle you want by giving, saving, and spending smart.

Born Saver Meets Born Spender

The 10/10/80 Rule

I'm a born saver. I was due on January 20 and born on December 28, just in time to give my dad another income tax deduction. My husband, Bob, on the other hand, was born two weeks late, on Mother's Day, which his mom spent in labor. He spent all her strength to come into this world and was dubbed a born spender.

If there's any doubt whether the name fits, I should tell you that Bob also spent his lunch money before he got to school. Don't get me wrong; he has a fabulous work ethic. But when he was a kid, his paper route money never saw the inside of his pocket. This pattern continued into his adult years, and when he became a fighter pilot in the air force, he could still spend money faster than his Stealth F-117 could go from zero to 500.

And then he met me.

I still have my lunch money from third grade.

So what happened when Bob the Spender met Ellie the Saver and carried her over the threshold?

Let me put it this way: Bob decided he'd rather volunteer for a two-week survival training exercise than come home and tell me that he forgot to use a coupon on the pizza he bought for dinner. He was more philosophical in his view of wealth. He figured if he worked hard, he could spend hard. I, on the other hand, was more practical. I also had so many rules and regulations for spending that I was an uptight bore.

So we had the basic issue of opposites attracting, and we had to find a way to marry our spending styles. Something amazing happened when we started to work through our differences. We discovered that if applied correctly, our polar approaches to money could *complete* rather than *compete*. Bob could balance me and I could balance him, and a marriage of two opposites really could lead to a rich life together.

The same is true for money matters. You need philosophical and practical smarts.

First, we have to explore the philosophical, and that is where the 10/10/80 Rule makes its entrance. If you live by this rule, you'll be rich. Period. No caveats, no secret handshakes, no need to spend another $89.99

for a special "10/10/80 Rule Implementation Kit." And your riches won't be in just dollars and cents, but in living and giving, in relationships and legacies.

The 10/10/80 Rule crosses all boundaries of religion, race, creed, and economic status. This rule is similar to the law of gravity. If you jump off a cliff, gravity kicks in even if you are screaming all the way down that two-hundred-foot drop, "I...don't...believe...in this...laaaaaaaw!" When the 10/10/80 Rule is applied to money, you have the secret for creating true riches, even if you don't believe in it.

The 10/10/80 Rule is simple:

- With the first 10 percent of your income, practice **The Rule of Giving 10 Percent.** The philosophy is that the *sweetest* dollar you ever make is the one you give away. The practical truth is, if you give away the first 10 percent, you'll have more coming in.

- With the next 10 percent of your income, practice **The Rule of Saving 10 Percent.** The philosophy is the *safest* dollar you ever make is the one you put away. The practical truth is, if you put it away, you'll have money for the future.

- Then practice **The Rule of Spending Smart** on that remaining 80 percent of your income. The philosophy here is the *smartest* dollar you ever make is the one you spend well. And the practical truth is that smart spending will allow you to live in your own home when the ARMs (adjustable rate mortgages) start to rise and house prices drop. It means a recession-proof life when the economy is shaky and consumer confidence is low. It means you'll have less stress because you've got good habits. When everyone else is panicking because food costs are on the rise, you'll already know the ins and outs of consistently finding good deals. These good habits carry you to the place where you can still take vacations even when gas is at sky-high prices. No matter what the economy, you can ride it like a gnarly wave handled by a skilled surfer and take it all the way to the shore standing up. It's a simple, straightforward strategy that works every time because if you spend wisely, you won't have debt, and that's the crux of spending smart. But you can completely blow this idea out of the water if you spend beyond your means.

Living Rich for Less demonstrates that these ideas are solid, tried, and true rules that worked for previous generations. We can bring these rules into our generation and the next, a generation that wants something more than the debt and stress their parents experienced.

Incorporating the 10/10/80 Rule into your lifestyle means living rich and could even be called the Bill Gates Rule or the Warren Buffet Rule. But there are some obstacles to this rule that I call Mutant Rules, and they can interfere with the rich life.

Mutant Rule 1: The 10/20/70 (or Born Saver) Rule

I like to bake for my family (and they don't complain). Sour cream pound cake with fresh strawberries and cream, homemade cappuccino brownies, dutch apple pie with strudel topping, and chocolate cake à la mode are some of our faves. This last dessert is my husband's favorite because the chocolate cake is served with vanilla ice cream and chocolate sauce. When it comes to chocolate sauce, Bob is of the philosophy that "if a little is good, a lot is better." His dessert ends up looking like a Hershey's Syrup truck collided with a Sara Lee truck—gooey and sloppy and won't win any awards for presentation.

Some people apply this same idea to putting money back into savings and investments, especially born savers. If you can save more than 10 percent (a little is good, a lot is better), that's great. There's certainly nothing wrong with saving 20 percent or more in order to reach certain financial goals. Some people even have accelerated savings strategies in order to buy a new home, open a business, retire before forty, or plan ahead for one income when children come along. All of these and more are viable reasons to go the route of aggressive savings.

I was born saving money and know what it's like to feel the compulsion to save, invest, and then save some more. But I needed to be brought into balance—especially when we had such a huge debt load and poor financial picture in our early marriage. Saving that kind of percentage wasn't realistic.

In fact, it's not realistic for the average person or family in mainstream America either. A 10/20/70 approach can set you up for failure when you're trying to achieve a savings plan beyond your ability—you can become a slave to saving money. And you can end up a frugal mess, a Scrooge, a cheapskate, a miser like Hetty Green.

Hetty was the richest woman in the world in 1916. She was so cheap that she wore her clothes until they became threadbare, ate warmed-up oatmeal, and wouldn't let her son, Ned, get medical treatment at the hospital when he broke his leg. Gangrene set in and Ned's leg was amputated.

Bizarre, I know, and an illustration that compulsive saving can turn you into a psycho freak.

I don't know about you, but I don't want any of those labels. I'd rather be called someone who is living rich for less.

The next danger of a 10/20/70 rule is the temptation to take that extra amount from your giving in order to keep up with an unrealistic investment strategy. It's another reason that the 10/20/70 rule doesn't generally work for most families.

You may move in and out of these rules at different times in your financial life, and that's cool too. If your spouse has a banner year in his or her employment and has some unexpected cash flowing, start saving more—it's smart. But remember that your budgeting and saving strategies must be fluid in order to accommodate any long-term goals. And over the long haul, ten, twenty, thirty years down the road, if you've stuck to the basic 10/10/80 Rule, then you will be living rich.

Mutant Rule 2: The 0/20/80 (or Selfish) Rule

This one could be called "The Selfish Rule," and it is in direct contrast to the 10/10/80 Rule. There are people who earn money to keep it and people who earn money to manage it and eventually give it away. Those who selfishly hold it close, choosing to build up investments rather than investing in their communities and other nonprofit organizations, end up with less in terms of quality of life than those who give it away. The "more" that 10/10/80 people end up with isn't always measured in dollars and cents, but sometimes it is! "More" is the idea that you are making a difference in the world and that it will be a better place because of how you've managed your money. The next chapter delves further into the first rule of money— giving.

Mutant Rule 3: The 10/10/90 Debt (or Born Spender) Rule

Oftentimes people try to manipulate the 10/10/80 Rule by adding more numbers and changing it into their own theory of spending. This is particularly true of born spenders. When you buy more house than you need because adjustable rate mortgages are low and housing prices are on the rise, you've manipulated the numbers and it won't work. It's not the 10/10/90 Rule—where you spend, in credit, 10 percent more than you earn.

Average consumer debt in the United States is steadily on the rise and currently stands at $8,500 per person. This doesn't include debt for a mortgage or car loans, only consumer and credit card debt. Here's an example of how our current culture takes the 10/10/80 Rule and turns it into the 10/10/90 Debt Rule. This chart shows that if you overspend your income by only $100 per month, in ten years you will be over $30,000 in debt:

Based on charging $100 to credit cards each month

Year	Amount Over Budget	Accumulated Interest	End-of-Year Debt
1	$1,200	$104	$1,304
2	1,200	463	2,863
3	1,200	1,128	4,728
4	1,200	2,157	6,957
5	1,200	3,621	9,621
6	1,200	5,608	12,808
7	1,200	8,217	16,617
8	1,200	11,572	21,172
9	1,200	15,818	26,618
10	1,200	21,129	33,129
11	1,200	27,714	40,914
12	1,200	35,821	50,221
13	1,200	45,749	61,349
14	1,200	57,855	74,655
15	1,200	72,562	90,562
Totals	$18,000	$72,562	$90,562

So Are You a Born Spender or a Born Saver?

If you believe that you are either a born spender or a born saver, then it's time to evaluate where you fit. Do you live to spend or spend to live? Are you so tight with a nickel that you give the president a constant migraine?

Born Saver Money Statements

In contrast to our Born Spender quiz on page 14, here are some smart money mantras that will put or keep some money in your pocket:

- "I have a modest mortgage because I want to own my house and not have my house own me."

- "I live by a reasonable budget and avoid using a home equity loan for consumer debt because it only deteriorates the equity in my home and borrows on my future. Besides, most people who use HELOCs to pay consumer debt are right back in that much debt within eighteen months."

- "I drive a nice car that was a year or two old when I bought it and was the best value according to Kbb.com and Edmunds.com. I refuse to finance my vehicle for so long that I would have negative equity in it."

- "We adjust our withholding so that we get our money during the year, invest it, and don't get a big tax refund."

- "I'm not going to borrow $10,000 from my 401(k)/IRA in order to pay off some of my consumer debt. The details indicate that the penalties and interest do not make it a cost-effective loan."

- "The market will leverage out in time, and building my 401(k) is still a good idea no matter what kind of market."

- "I don't make emotional investments, like investing in a company because of either panic or euphoria based on reading the newspaper. But I do invest in companies about which I know the goods and services of that industry and can gauge when the company is doing well or poorly."

- "I always try to contribute to a nondeductible IRA or Roth IRA because there is a long-term tax benefit."

- "Refinancing when closing costs are at a minimum and I can save 1.5 percent in interest is a good move and worth the inconvenience. It's often a perceived hassle and not a genuine problem."

- "The little choices add up to big ones at the grocery store. For example, this week I purchased Dawn Ultra because it contains 30 percent more cleaning ingredients per drop than the leading non-concentrated brand, and unlike some larger bottles of dish liquid that have more water, with Dawn Ultra, I get what I pay for—more power, not more water. With Dawn Ultra, I can clean more dishes without the water feeling greasy."

(Look on the front of a nickel.) There has to be a balance between this compulsion to spend or save—a healthy balance that leads to rich living.

We all make mistakes and poor choices, but certain patterns lead to wealth and certain patterns lead to poverty—no matter how much money you make. There's also the need for balance—you shouldn't strive to be a 100 percent born saver or a 100 percent born spender. Whether you're already rich or whether you're poor, you will become the sum of your money choices.

Our wealth is usually in an ever-changing state and should be viewed as a fluid condition. Most of us are in process and few have really arrived. One area of our money management will usually need tweaking. The guy in the $3,500 Armani suit watching CNBC has as much to learn about how to teach his kids the value of a buck as the middle-aged woman buying a $1.89 iced sugar-free vanilla coffee at McDonald's. (Cha Ching! She just saved $2—the same drink at Starbucks costs $3.89.) Mr. Armani's kids may never learn how to manage money and end up in serious credit card debt as a result. Or Ms. McDonald's might have kids that go to Stanford on full scholarships after learning the values she taught them about working for what they want. Or Mr. Armani might effectively raise the next Warren Buffet, and Ms. McDonald's kids might end up on welfare. There are no limitations on wise or stupid money choices.

Smart money decisions will lead to wealth. Habitual, stupid money decisions can lead to a lifetime of payback. Paying back creditors, paying ex-spouses (divorced over money arguments—the number one reason for divorce), and a payback of no retirement funds for your golden years.

Take the Born Spender Quiz

So how do you know if you're a born spender or a born saver when it comes to basic money issues? The following are typical born spender statements. Note whether you agree, disagree, or are unsure about each of these money statements.

_____ "I have a very large mortgage because all mortgage debt is good debt."

_____ "I don't need to have a budget. I'll just use a home equity loan to pay off credit card debt."

_____ "I'll put it on my credit card. Even if I can't pay it off at the end of the month, I'll get it paid off in time."

_____ "I need to drive a really nice/new car because it will save on maintenance."

_____ "We always get a big tax refund."

_____ "I'm going to borrow from my 401(k)/IRA. I'll look into the details later."

_____ "I'm not building my 401(k) in this kind of market."

_____ "I like/invest in this company because I know it."

_____ "I don't want to contribute to a nondeductible IRA because there's no tax benefit."

_____ "I should probably refinance, but it really seems like a hassle."

Give yourself one point for every question you answered agree, two points for unsure, and three points for disagree. Now rate yourself according to the following.

Big Born Spender

If you scored less than 18, you clearly have a born spender's mentality toward finances. You really need advice from a financial counselor or other born saver who can help you reach balance in this area. You need to take deliberate, disciplined action to overcome this approach to money management, because if you continue down the path you're currently on, you'll likely end up in need of some kind of bailout or may even end up filing for bankruptcy. With this philosophy, you'll likely have little to no retirement funds in your golden years or positive financial future to pass on to your children. But there's still hope for your future. I married a born spender, and he's been converted into a guy who has a solid grip on money.

Born Spender

If you scored between 18 and 22, you're susceptible to making bad money moves that could keep you in debt for most of your life. You most likely live above your means and have a mounting debt problem. It would be wise to develop a better understanding of money management and begin a path toward the right attitudes and actions that will help you improve your financial status.

Saver/Spender

If you scored between 22 and 26, you're pretty balanced. There are a few areas where you could make slightly better money choices, but you probably enjoy your life and have the financial freedom to be able to live a rich lifestyle. All you need to do is tweak your choices here and there to maintain balance and build a little bit more security.

Born Saver

If you scored between 26 and 30, you're a born saver. Before you salsa dance in celebration, keep in mind that maxing out this score could possibly indicate a lack of balance in some areas. Do you give away your resources on a regular basis? Are you generous with your time and money? If you can answer "yes" to these questions, then you're very likely right where you need to be to get the gold star. You still need to be careful that you don't obsess about saving and take the time to enjoy a rich lifestyle.

I fall into this category, and I constantly have to reevaluate my spending to make sure I take those family vacations, buy more underwear before they become holey, and learn to splurge a bit here and there to really enjoy life.

Living Rich Questions

Are you a Born Spender or a Born Saver?
How many born saver statements are you willing to adopt as your own?

Part 1

Giving 10 Percent

The sweetest dollar you ever make is the one you give away

"Begin with the end in mind." That's what Stephen Covey told us more than twenty years ago. I remember the first time I heard the concept. I was in my college economics class, and our professor was reading from Covey's book. I was trying to act all intelligent and cerebral over this first habit of highly effective people. I pursed my lips, adjusted the huge padded shoulders on my jacket, and ran my fingers through my big Texas hair, trying very hard to look thoughtful and contemplative.

I'm afraid I only succeeded in looking like a Dallas Cowboys cheerleader who had just been told that all Paul Mitchell hairspray products had been recalled for being environmentally unsafe. In other words, I tried to understand, but I clearly didn't have a clue. Begin with the end in mind? What in the wide world of sports did *that* mean? *How can you get all the way to the end—first? How do you know where to begin?*

Eventually the professor's assistant explained it all to me, using small words and drawing pictures. I learned to imagine the end goal and then take the steps needed to get there. Once you know what's at the other end of the journey, you're more likely to arrive. Even a very young, big-haired Texas woman living in the overstimulated eighties could learn that concept.

My "end" has always been about people. I was a born saver but also a born giver. I made my parents so mad when I gave away my dolls and fund-raising candy bars. I wanted to give everything I could to help people reach their own end—but I had to learn the best way to give. So this first section is all about the big give—how to do it smart, how to want to do it, and how to do it in a way that allows you and others to prosper in the process.

This first section, the idea of giving your first 10 percent, is what sets apart the average from the super–above average folks. How many "givers" do you know who are perpetually poor? Not many. You'll find out how giving can bring out the superhero in you. When Mr. and Ms. America give—the sky's the limit.

In short, give and you'll be rich. I'll show you how. That's the end we're looking toward—so that's where we'll begin.

1

Little Miss Giver

Giving It Away Will Make You Rich

If you want to live rich, then you give
what you can and start where you are.

ELLIE KAY

One of our favorite movies is *¡Three Amigos!*, which features a set of actors in the 1930s who are down on their luck. They end up in Mexico with a situation of mistaken identity. Steve Martin (Lucky Day), Chevy Chase (Dusty Bottoms), and Martin Short (Ned Nederlander) deliver some of the best comedic performances of their careers.

At the beginning of the movie, they get a telegram from a poor village in Santa Poco asking them to come rescue them from the villain, El Guapo.

LUCKY DAY [reading telegram]: "Three Amigos, Hollywood, California. You are very great. 100,000 pesos. Come to Santa Poco put on show. Stop. The In-famous El Guapo."

DUSTY BOTTOMS: What does that mean, in-famous?

NED NEDERLANDER: Oh, Dusty. In-famous is when you're *more* than famous. This man El Guapo, he's not just famous, he's IN-famous.

LUCKY DAY: 100,000 pesos to perform with this El Guapo, who's
    probably the biggest actor to come out of Mexico!
DUSTY BOTTOMS: Wow, in-famous? In-famous?

Wouldn't each of us like to be famous for something?

When I was seven years old, I ended up as the "infamous money kid"
at Atwood Elementary School in Fort Worth, Texas. It all started one
morning when I poured cereal into my bowl, and out of the box popped
destiny in the form of a hand buzzer. You wound up the buzzer, hid it, and
then when you shook someone's hand, you *buzzed* them. I was delighted
with the potential this incredible prize held and debated shaking my mom's
hand. Then I thought about the new paddleball my brother had just gotten from our grandma and the fact that as soon as the string broke, Mom
would use the paddle for another reason. I decided against buzzing her.
Instead, I used that novelty item to set up my first business. Before school,
at recess, and after school, I set up "Ellie's Electrifying Handshakes"—girls
could get buzzed for a nickel, and boys could get a shock for only fifteen
cents. I charged the boys more because of the cootie factor. I felt I should
be compensated for the risk of catching those conspicuous cooties.

My marketing plan included two-for-one deals and frequent-buyer programs. When these tactics didn't work, I had a secret weapon: the double-
dog dare for the kids who were afraid of the shock. That one worked every
time. These marketing techniques were so successful that in only two weeks,
I made $10. That was a lot of handshakes! I stored my stash in a little plas-
tic butter bowl filled with nickels and dimes. When I proudly showed my
mom my buzz stash, she smiled and said, "Great job! You need to know that
$1 of that $10 goes in the offering plate on Sunday morning."

What? I thought. *I can't keep all my money? I gotta give some away? But
it's mine!*

That was my first introduction to the idea of a tithe, or 10 percent that goes out as a gift. I remember Mrs. Rickards, my Sunday school teacher, telling us that our offerings were going to children in Africa. Even though I didn't like the idea of having to give away my own money, I did like the idea of trying to help those kids. That next Sunday, in the seven-year-olds' classroom, Mrs. Rickards passed a shiny gold plate with red felt in the center. The other kids dropped in nickels, dimes, and a few quarters. When the plate was handed to me, I proudly put in my hard-earned dollar bill.

Then something happened to me that I'll never forget.

My imagination was as infamous as my ability to make money, and suddenly I thought of those dark-faced kids with the swollen stomachs I'd seen in pictures during our lesson. I imagined how my dollar would give those kids good food; they might even gain some weight and become healthy again. I pictured what those sad faces would look like when a missionary handed them food. My dollar would make the difference between life and death for them. In my mind's eye, they smiled, laughed as they took the food and ate it. In the heart of Africa, those nourished children would stand up and slowly begin to dance. At that moment, a rush of tears came to my eyes, and I got goose bumps. I realized something:

The sweetest dollar that I'd ever earned
was the one I could give away.

It suddenly didn't matter that I couldn't keep all my money. I *wanted* to give it away—my earnings had a purpose. From that week on, I worked hard, and in one way or another, every month I mailed money to Africa. This lasted from the time I was seven until I graduated high school, and the donation increased as my earning potential increased. It continues today as well with Bob and me and our family. During times of financial prosperity and during times of financial challenge, we've always given away at least 10 percent of our earned income.

Here's what we did with this first part of the 10/10/80 Rule:

- Even though we had $40,000 in consumer debt when we married, we knew we still needed to follow the rule of giving.
- Even though my husband took a $15,000-a-year pay cut to go into the air force while I chose to stay home with the kids, we gave.
- Even though we had five more babies in seven years, for a total of seven children to support, we gave.
- Even though we barely had enough money in those first few years to buy groceries, we still gave.

Here are the results of following this rule:

- We never went hungry.
- Our children were never beggars.
- Our finances were not ever forsaken.
- We got out of debt.
- We lived well.
- Our kids will graduate college debt free.
- We never regretted a dollar given.

Five Steps to Rich and Infamous

Bob and I developed an "infamous" ability to handle money, and it helped us get out of debt and stay out of debt, but it also did much more. It led to a lifestyle, a way of living, that enabled our family, even though we were supporting seven children on one military paycheck, to gain a substantial quality of life.

Over the course of the next fifteen years (long before I started making money as a writer), we were able to pay cash for eleven cars (and give away three of those), buy a nice five-bedroom home, go on family vacations, dress well and live well, and remain free from consumer debt. We were also able to donate to more than thirty nonprofit organizations around the world that helped feed the hungry, shelter the homeless, and make a few kids smile and dance. During our first fifteen years of marriage, we gave over $100,000 to these nonprofit groups. This is living rich, to help others live a richer life as well.

Plus we've been able to raise kids who know how to live rich as well. Rather than a generational downward spiral, we've been able to change that mold into an upward cycle. This helps our kids, the next generation, start their adult lives from a much better position than we started ours.

The 10/10/80 Rule: Why Sharing Matters

I was quoted in a front-page story in *USA Today* as saying, "It was all about keeping up with the Joneses. Now, the Joneses are starting to cut back." Saving and giving money has become the new cool. But there's nothing new about it to me!

This is something I've been preaching from the beginning, ten years ago. In my first book, *Shop, Save, and Share,* I wrote that the heart of the message was the "sharing" element, or being a provision to others in need. More and more of the top financial experts, such as David Bach, Jean Chatsky, Suze Orman, and Dave Ramsey, are seeing the value of giving away a part of their wealth in an effort to find balance in life. They all recommend the tithe or a portion that is given.

There's more benefit for those who live rich than just good tax breaks; the value lies in the pure joy of giving. According to the Merrill Lynch/ Capgemini report, millionaires who live in North America are two to five times more likely to give to causes they value than their European cousins. You don't have to be a millionaire to give either. In fact, 70 percent of

American households gave some money away last year. In 2006, Americans gave almost 2 percent of our GDP (gross domestic product), which was about $300 billion, to three different areas:

- **Church:** Place of worship or affiliated activities
- **Crisis:** A local or worldwide emergency, such as a hurricane or tsunami, or a crisis such as a child needing surgery the family cannot afford
- **Community:** Local fund-raising efforts in the community by a group the donor is associated with[1]

The Big Givers

The two biggest givers in the modern world are also the two richest: Bill and Melinda Gates, and Warren Buffet. The Gateses set up a foundation that would donate $35 billion to address significant worldwide issues such as education, health care, hunger, and poverty. Warren Buffet endowed the Gates Foundation with $30 billion, the bulk of his fortune. When asked why he gave it to the foundation, he replied, "I got rich because investors thought I could make more investing their money than they could. Bill and Melinda can spend my money better than I could."[2]

There's something contagious about giving, and major personalities are getting into the giving groove. Bill Clinton wrote the book *Giving: How Each of Us Can Change the World.* Oprah's reality show, *Oprah's Big Give,* featured contestants who wanted to "do good and give back," where the winner was the biggest giver.

Guess what? We don't have to let Bill Clinton and Oprah Winfrey be the best givers in the world. In fact, each of us can give like a celebrity— take a few steps back and look at giving in accordance with your earnings or ability to give.

Giving like the Rich and Famous

In researching this section on giving, I wanted to think about what it would feel like to be able to give like the rich and famous. Then I thought about equivalents and asked myself the question: If I gave $100 to a third-world child, what would that look like, in proportional income, to what Julia Roberts could give? I found a fascinating link to a celebrity calculator that helped me develop that line of thought a bit further. If you go to the Links page on my Web site, you can further explore this concept with your favorite celebrity. (See www.ellieKay.com)

Look at what Mr. and Ms. America pay in proportion to Mr. and Ms. Celebrity. Based on annual earnings of various celebrities, the chart tells us what certain items seem to cost for an average American:

Tobey Maguire
Annual Income: $4,000,000

Product	At This Price	Seems to Cost
House	$275,000.00	$2,062.50
Car	$20,000.00	$150.00
Laptop	$2,000.00	$15.00
Hotel Room	$100.00	$0.75
Average Meal	$10.00	$0.08
Big Mac	$2.29	$0.02

Kirsten Dunst
Annual Income: $8,000,000

Product	At This Price	Seems to Cost
House	$275,000.00	$1,031.25
Car	$20,000.00	$75.00

Product	At This Price	Seems to Cost	(cont.)
Laptop	$2,000.00	$7.50	
Hotel Room	$100.00	$0.38	
Average Meal	$10.00	$0.04	
Big Mac	$2.29	$0.01	

George Clooney
Annual Income: $15,000,000

Product	At This Price	Seems to Cost
House	$275,000.00	$550.00
Car	$20,000.00	$40.00
Laptop	$2,000.00	$4.00
Hotel Room	$100.00	$0.20
Average Meal	$10.00	$0.02
Big Mac	$2.29	$0.00

Julia Roberts
Annual Income: $25,000,000

Product	At This Price	Seems to Cost
House	$275,000.00	$330.00
Car	$20,000.00	$24.00
Laptop	$2,000.00	$2.40
Hotel Room	$100.00	$0.12
Average Meal	$10.00	$0.00
Big Mac	$2.29	$0.00

It costs the average American a lot to be generous at average earning levels, and this celebrity calculator shows that.[3] First and foremost, take note that some people make more money than George Clooney. But this calculator also shows that when most of us would donate $4 to the American Cancer Society in average earning money, George Clooney would have to donate $2,000 of his earning power to keep up with our level of generosity. Or if I gave $100 to support a third-world child, Julia Roberts would have to give $83,000 to be as proportionally generous as I am!

It only stands to reason that the money earned and donated by mainstream America is even more valuable than a lot of the donations by celebrities. Think about that the next time you tip $11 for a meal that cost you $50. Just remember that if Tobey Maguire wanted to keep up with you, he'd have to tip $1,466. And if Kirsten Dunst were to leave the same tip you did, it would be like she left six pennies on the table. You really are one big giver after all.

Start Where You Are, Give What You Can

Although it is interesting to compare ourselves to the rich and famous, it can also lead to frustration and feelings of futility. Do our meager monetary donations really matter?

Yes, and in a big way. All you have to do is go to a third-world country for a few days to see how much the average American lives like a celebrity compared to others around the world. When I went to China, a massage that would cost me $90 in America only cost $3. That means that the $3 I donate to reputable groups working in China would have $90 of earning power. A $3,000 donation to Mission of Joy, a charity we sponsor in India, builds an entire floor of an orphanage—the equivalent of $300,000 here!

Your monetary donations, humble as they may seem to you, not only go further to help others around the world, they have another benefit that is amazing. While giving does something significant for others, sometimes

Quick-Time Tax Time

- A family filing married jointly, making $65,000 and tithing $6,500 (in the 25 percent tax bracket) would see an estimated tax savings benefit of around $1,625 if they reach the itemized minimum.
- A single person donating $1,500 in January instead of December and another $3,950 throughout the next year (in cash and other donations) would usually reach the minimum to itemize. If in the 15 percent bracket, he or she would then save approximately $900 in taxes.
- A married couple filing jointly in the 33 percent tax bracket could donate $8,000 in tithes and another $3,000 in household item donations to nonprofit organizations, such as Goodwill or Salvation Army, in order to save a total of $3,597 in taxes. Sometimes setting up this kind of additional giving standard in addition to your other cash and household item donations can lower your overall taxable income to the point where you are in a lower tax bracket—thereby saving even more on your taxes.
- Your kids' donations would count toward the overall donations as well. In an itemized package, a family in the 25 percent bracket with three children donating $100 each would see an approximate tax benefit of $75 savings.

the greater good is what it does for the giver. By giving money, you free yourself to bring life into your finances. You begin to realize that starting where you are, in terms of tithing, is better than not starting at all. You also realize that giving what you can is better than ignoring your conscience and giving nothing at all. Because when you give, you gain far more. When you hoard, you die inside. It's a basic principle that takes its name from a sea of salt in the Middle East between Jordan and Israel.

Learn from the Dead Sea

The Dead Sea is 1,378 feet below sea level, and its shores are the lowest point on dry land on the surface of the earth. Its saline levels are around 30 percent, and consequently no fish or sea creatures are able to live in this body of water. Even though fresh water empties into the Dead Sea, it is dead to all life because there is no outlet. The fresh water begins to thicken with salt and eventually becomes as dead as the rest of the sea—all because there is no outlet.

This principle applies to the spiritual aspect of our finances when we give into our lower natures—although money is coming in, nothing is going out to help others. Just as laws of nature are evident in the Dead Sea, spiritual laws of money stewardship can empower us to live rich by following the most basic of these laws: the law of giving. On the other hand, when we lose our desire to help people in those three major areas where most Americans give—church, crisis, and community—we lose the spiritual vitality of our financial life.

Let me put it in personal and practical terms. Bob and I were sorely tempted to ignore the first part of the 10/10/80 Rule and not give when we had that $40,000 in debt and couldn't make ends meet. But we truly believed in the spiritual aspect of giving: by sharing that first 10 percent, we would always be taken care of financially. It doesn't always add up quantitatively, but that doesn't mean it is exclusively anecdotal. In other words, you can't always measure spiritual truth on the bottom line of a spreadsheet. You have to allow for the faith factor, which may not show up on the front end of a chart or graph or formula. But in our experience, it always showed up on the bottom line.

If we hoarded, we died financially, but when we opened up that channel of giving, we found new life. Sometimes it showed up in the most
amazing ways, like when I won the main prize on a game show and we
sold it for cash. Other times it was manifested in a humbling way—like
when people gave us clothing that exactly fit our children and was a perfect provision.

No matter how many charts, graphs, diagrams, numbers, and formulas you read in this book, one of the most powerful measurements cannot
really be gauged in dollars and cents. The measurement of living rich is
often reflected in giving rich—and that, my friend, is a matter of faith.

Give like a Millionaire

As an exercise in creativity and to begin thinking like a big giver, fill in the
last column of the chart below. The Tobey Maguire income is in the "seems
to cost" column. If by writing a check for $150 you could buy someone a
car (not you or your family), who would you choose?

Tobey Maguire

Annual Income: $4,000,000   **(Example)**

Product	*At This Price*	*Seems to Cost*	*I Would Donate to…*
House	$275,000.00	$2,062.50	Mission of Joy
Car	$20,000.00	$150.00	ELIC (China)
Laptop	$2,000.00	$15.00	Jumpstart (community)
Hotel Room	$100.00	$0.75	local homeless shelter
Average Meal	$10.00	$0.08	World Vision
Big Mac	$2.29	$0.02	The Hunger Project (global)

Now go back and look at the amounts in the "seems to cost" column
again. If you were to tithe 10 percent of your income, how close could you

get to making a difference in those three primary areas: church, crisis, and community?

Give Money Wisely

In recent years, the total amount of money Americans have donated is roughly $260 billion a year! These dollars help millions of people world-wide. While I think it's important to give to your own community, we've seen from the charts what an incredible impact American money can have on third-world nations. When asked why they don't sponsor a child or give to a national or global charity, most people will say they aren't certain that their money really goes to that child or that program. Some of the greatest concerns are also very legitimate: the idea that donations go to fund-raising efforts, to overhead, or to large executive salaries. The answer for this concern is very simple: Go to the Better Business Bureau Wise Giving Alliance at Give.org for the BBB *Wise Giving Guide*. This will help you decide which organization to choose.

Don't Fund Overhead or Fund-Raising

There are two main areas to look at when considering where your dollars will go in your tithe. Here are the red flags that indicate caution:

- **Overhead.** An organization I researched was a common name I'd donated to on several occasions, but they used 85 percent for over-head costs.
- **Fund-Raising.** Excessive expenses associated with raising more money is a major red flag as well. Some organizations channel as much as 90 percent of their donations toward fund-raising. On the other hand, there are other organizations where as much as 90 percent of your dollar goes toward relief and not internal programs.

Know the Details on Major Donations

It's one thing to donate to a community fund-raiser on occasion, but it's quite another to regularly commit funds to a long-term charity commitment. The BBB Wise Giving Alliance offers guidance to donors on making informed giving decisions through their charity evaluations, various "tips" publications, and the quarterly *Wise Giving Guide*. You can access this information by calling (703) 276-0100 or going to Give.org.

You can ask them to send you the various tip guides by mail, or read online about topics such as

- Charitable giving
- Police and firefighter organizations
- Handling unwanted direct mail from charitable organizations
- Child sponsorship organizations
- Direct mail sweepstakes and charities
- Contributing used cars to charities
- Tax deductions for charitable contributions

Give the Gift of Life to a Third-World Child

Most sponsorships run anywhere from $25 to $35 per month and provide food, clothing, housing, medical care, and education to children. We've had the thrill of watching kids grow up under our sponsorship and go on to become leaders in their communities. Our family currently sponsors children from three reputable organizations:

- **World Vision.** On their "Ways to Give" link, you can choose where you want your dollars to go. World Vision helps children in the United States as well as around the world. Go to World vision.org, or call (888) 511-6598.
- **Compassion International.** This organization is tuned in to crisis and special needs as well as the general monthly needs of children around the world. They encourage communication with your

child, and you have the chance to see photos and how the child is doing in school. It's a great project for your family. Their Web site is Compassion.com.

- **Mission of Joy.** This is a lesser-known organization that was started by two air force captains when they saw the needs in India. Twenty years later, thousands of people have been positively impacted by this nonprofit organization. Almost 97 percent of the monthly contributions go directly to India because the ministry uses volunteer help and has very little overhead. Go to Missionofjoy.org.

Giving Tax-Smart

Please note that any discussions on taxes are based on a number of detailed factors that change from year to year and person to person. As always, you should check with your tax professional before making any financial decisions that will impact your overall tax liability.

- **Donations to your local church and community.** Your local church body helps teach your family spiritual values, runs kids' programs in the summers, provides food and clothing to orphanages, and sends money to victims of natural disasters. If you aren't a part of a local church, you and your family are missing out on some incredible opportunities. According to Barna Research Online (Barna.org), Americans believe in the power and impact of prayer: More than four out of five adults (82 percent) pray during a typical week. Four out of five (82 percent) believe that "prayer can change what happens in a person's life." Nine out of ten adults (89 percent) agree that "there is a God who watches over you and answers your prayers." Almost nine out of ten people (87 percent) say that the universe was originally created by God. If Americans are open to the idea of God, then why not find a church that meets your family's unique spiritual needs? Once you find your fit, partner with them financially to reach your community.

- **Double up.** But what if you're just getting started and don't think you'll have enough deductions to itemize on your income tax return? You could double up on your giving by deferring the year-end gifts that would normally be given in December until January of the new year. Then give your regular gifts at the end of that year too. This "doubling up" will likely give you the amount you need to itemize.

- **Record keeping.** If you itemize, it is critical that you get tax-deductible receipts for all donations to any nonprofit organization, including Goodwill, the Salvation Army, Vietnam Veterans of America, Military Order of the Purple Heart, homeless shelters, and other agency thrift shops. Money donated directly to a needy person is not deductible. It would be better to donate the amount to your church anonymously and have them send the donation to the family in need. Check with your tax specialist every year for your state and federal tax laws.

- **Start your own foundation.** If you are fortunate enough to have a large gain from a stock or mutual fund that you have held for over a year, consider using it to become what is essentially your own foundation. For example, if you own $5,000 worth of stock that you bought years ago for only $1,000, you can donate the stock by setting up a Fidelity Charitable Gift Fund account (call [800] 682-4438, or go to Charitablegift.org). By doing this, you get an immediate $5,000 tax deduction and save having to pay taxes on the $4,000 gain. In the years to come, as that $5,000 grows, you can instruct the company that manages your founda-tion where to donate the proceeds. Besides Fidelity, charitable gift funds are also available through Vanguard at (888) 383-4483 or Vanguardcharitable.org, or Schwab at (800) 746-6216 or Schwabcharitable.org.

- **Kid philanthropists.** You may want to allow your children to manage a donation of a predetermined amount ($25, $50, $100, or whatever you have budgeted). They get to research a variety of nonprofit organizations and decide which one will receive their donation. Then donate the amount in your child's name. You get the tax benefit, your child gets the thank-you note, and you both feel good about giving.

Living Rich Questions

Would you *consider* giving away *a part* of your income/assets on a regular basis? (We're not asking for a commitment at this point, just consideration of the concept.)

If you knew your monetary tithe would have the scope and impact of the monies donated by a movie star, where would you give and why?

Where have you given in the past, and where would you like to start giving in the future?

2

Little Moneybags Grows Up

Four Ways to Give like a Child

The fortune which nobody sees makes
a person happy and unenvied.
FRANCIS BACON

After Ellie's Electrifying Handshakes was shut down in its third week of business because of an operations glitch (the buzzer broke), the CEO decided there were plenty more ways to give, save, and earn. During one of my summer breaks, I bought candy bars at the local discount drugstore and sold them door to door at a 100 percent markup. I figured there was intrinsic value in the product coming direct to the customer instead of the client having to get in the car, drive to the store, grab some choco, and get back home in time to start dinner. During my business hours, I found a couple of kids in the neighborhood whose dads were out of work, so I gave them a couple of the smaller bars for free. It felt good.

Another year I sold my Spanish grandmother's vegetables door to door. *Abuela* had an evil eye she would put on me if I refused to help market these valued veggies—so I had no choice. I had no problem working independently, but my girlfriend Dee Dee wanted to help and really needed the money since her parents were going through a divorce. So I made her a minor partner and gave her 20 percent of the profits. We sold out each week by taking the freshest produce around the neighborhood in my red Radio Flyer wagon. It felt good to teach someone else about business, sharing my entrepreneurial talents. Dee Dee was very appreciative and used the money to buy her mom a birthday present, a mood ring. Her mom was so touched she cried, which made the ring turn black.

In my later grade school years I established Ellie's Elegant Critters and cashed in on the popularity of *The Beverly Hillbillies* television show. I marketed the product to replace the Pet Rock that was famous at the time and produced hundreds of these creations made out of blue fake fur and plastic wiggly eyes. I spent an entire year on that business—investing hundreds of hours of my time.

Around this time my dad chimed in and began to call me his "little moneybags." I earned enough money to pay for a trip to Spain to visit my cousins. Of course, it wasn't my idea to spend the money; I wanted to save it in the bank. After all, I'd spent an entire year earning that cash and felt it was unfair of my folks to impose their will on my twelve-year-old self. But my folks began talking about how excited they were that I would have the chance to see my Spanish relatives and that at least one person in the family would have the privilege of going to Spain that summer. It seemed to mean so much to them. Besides, Abuela's garden was coming in, and she was already giving me the evil eye about selling door to door throughout another hot Texas summer. I figured if I changed my attitude and accepted my fate, I could please my parents and beat it out of town in time to avoid selling acres of the vegetables. It was a great two-for-one deal if I ever heard of one.

Through those early years and every opportunity to earn money, I learned something new about giving:

- I could give *things* like chocolate to kids who couldn't afford it.
- I could give *talents* by teaching Dee Dee a skill she didn't have.

- I could give *time* by dedicating an entire year to one business whose profits would fund a trip that was not my choosing.
- I could give my *'tude* and make my parents happy by having the right attitude.

Question: When is the last time you gave away something besides money, such as things, talents, and time (and had the right 'tude about it)? Write down these four categories, and think of all the ways you've given these gifts in the past month.

Giving like a Child

As you answer the questions for this chapter, you will either be surprised at how much you are already giving or embarrassed that you haven't had the time or desire to do very much giving in any of these areas.

I've found that the best way to give in these four critical areas is to tap into your inner child. Or think about how you used to give spontaneously as a kid and never thought anything about it. Yes, it's true that little humans can be as selfish as their grown-up counterparts, but most of them have their moments of generosity. I remember when my younger brother, Wally, was five years old. I loved it when Abuela gave him a candy bar (as the only boy, he was the favorite grandchild). I would ask him for some as soon as he got it (and Abuela was safely away in her garden). He would immediately break his Hershey's bar in two and give me the larger piece. He never even thought about it. At ten years old, I thought he was naive, but I got more chocolate and that's all I cared about.

A couple years later Wally had grown up, and the only way I could get chocolate out of him was to threaten to tell Mom that he sneaked into the freezer while she was at the grocery store and had eaten two packages of Twinkies and Ding Dongs. (Mom used to freeze them for school snacks, but he ate them anyway.) It worked every time.

A couple of lessons can be learned from my extortion experience: We can either give out of the goodness of our heart—generously, willingly, and spontaneously. Or we can find ourselves in a situation where we are giving grudgingly, unwillingly, and infrequently. But when you give like a child, you experience the irrefutable joy of giving. All you have to do is to give what you can and start where you are.

So where do you begin?

Giving Things

There are some very practical ways you can begin to start where you are and give what you can. I challenge you to follow-up on one item (just one) from each of the following areas for six weeks. You will find, especially if you haven't been giving very much, that contentment loves to walk alongside generosity.

My challenge is simply this: I believe you'll feel and live better after you begin a habit of giving. You'll be more content with what you have. You'll want to be more generous in what you choose to give. Try it for six weeks and see what happens.

- **Simplify!** One of the best ways to help yourself and others at the same time is to tackle a room, a closet, or even a piece of furniture and clean it out. In other words, get a bit more organized. I recommend investing in a good organizing book such as Marcia Ramsland's *Simplify Your Space: Create Order and Reduce Stress.* For example, you could choose to start in one of the bedrooms and go through dresser drawers. Take everything out of each drawer, and put each item in one of three piles: 1) GIVE AWAY, 2) THROW AWAY, and 3) KEEP.
- **Call a nonprofit organization that needs and wants your donations.** Some will even come pick up your donations. In

the process, you'll be helping meet the needs of other people in your community. Be sure to ask for an itemized receipt, and keep track of the original value and the donated value of the items for tax purposes. You'll need a receipt as proof for any donation over $250, but I recommend getting receipts on everything anyway. If you do this with each room in your home (including the garage), not only will you address the clutter, you'll relieve stress in the process while helping others. Does it get any better than that?

- **Donate.** Pay attention to information in your community about specific needs. This might be on flyers, in the newspaper, posted on a bulletin board, or in an interoffice memo. Don't ignore these needs. Instead dedicate fifteen minutes toward collecting specific items that are needed. If you gather only a few things, it will still help. It might be a matter of collecting your soda cans, gathering food items, or looking for specific items of clothing. You might even want to add some of these things to your shopping list and pick them up. If you begin to develop the mind-set of giving, the next time you hear of a need, you won't be inclined to think, *Oh no! Not again,* but rather, *I wonder how I can meet this need?* You don't have to be extravagant; it really is true that every little bit helps. Just give what you can and start where you are.

Give Away a Tenth of Everything

I've found that when you begin to hold your material goods in open palms rather than clenched fists, you'll discover all kinds of opportunities to be generous. One time a friend of mine got a food voucher because her flight was delayed. She'd already eaten, so she redeemed the coupon for five free gourmet cookies. She ended up giving three of them to fellow passengers who didn't have time to get lunch (cookies for lunch are better than no lunch at all, don't you think?). She gave away 60 percent of her food that day and felt so good about it. The mind-set was to meet someone's needs.

Here's a list of items you could give away, as well as examples from real people.

Clothing

Rather than selling clothes in a garage sale or on eBay, why not give them directly to people who can use them or to the Salvation Army or Goodwill? That's what Heather, from California, learned, and she got a major bonus in the process! She shares:

> My husband and I were having the same fights over and over again. It was all about the dreaded topic of money. He thought I didn't try hard enough, and I thought he spent money foolishly. Then we started to learn how to save money in order to share with others. Ellie really challenged us to make some drastic changes. Those changes transformed our life for the better! We realized we truly could cut corners in ways that weren't too painful. It truly wasn't that difficult to shave hundreds of dollars off our monthly budget and simplify other areas of our lives. One of the areas in which we helped ourselves and helped others was to simplify by going through our family's clothes. We gathered up a dozen boxes of clothes to pass along to people who needed them and donated them to Goodwill. By reaching out to others, we've taken the focus off ourselves and our (former) problems. My husband really appreciates the teamwork philosophy. Our marriage is better than it has been in a long time, and we don't argue about money all the time.

You don't have to be wealthy or even well-off in order to give. You can start where you are and give what you can, like single mom Ursula Mixon from Tulsa, Oklahoma, who got hooked on sharing. She wrote our offices:

Hi, Ellie! This is the first time I've accessed your Web site. I'm a single mother of two with a determination to eliminate debt. I used to say that I didn't have the time it took to figure out how to save money on a lot of the things we needed. I really didn't think I had anything to give to other people because it seemed like I was always the needy one. But now I realize that the hours I spend working overtime on my job I could be using to save money and spend more time with my children. But even better than that was the first time I started going through my maternity clothes and decided to donate them to a crisis pregnancy center. About a month later, I saw a teen mom in Wal-Mart wearing my donated top and jeans. I recognized them because they were really cute on her. She looked so happy, and it made me feel happy on the inside. Here I thought I was the needy one, and I ended up helping meet someone else's need. Thanks for the insight!

Food

All kinds of food drives go on regularly in your community. The post office has an annual Stamp Out Hunger campaign, the Boy Scouts collect canned goods, and there's always the local homeless shelter or food pantry. Sometimes giving away food before it exceeds the shelf life is a lot better than throwing it out. Here is what a man named Stephen, from Columbus, Mississippi, experienced:

A man named Peter from our church had been out of work for quite some time. He'd been applying for jobs week after week. We watched him diligently pursue job interviews to no avail as his sense of worth plummeted. One day we felt led to anonymously donate about eight bags of groceries to his family and left them on the doorstep.

The next week Peter came to church and publicly shared a moving story. He said his daughter had signed up to bring a cake to the school carnival. He knew they couldn't afford the cake mix, frosting, and oil. That afternoon he found the bags of groceries someone had quietly left on their porch. Inside the bag was a cake mix that required only water and frosting. Peter told us, "My hope had failed as I cried out to God and asked, *Why can't I find a job? Don't You care about me, God?* Then I had provision for these little needs, and when He did, I realized He cared about all my needs too."

Stephen wrote back later to say: "Peter found work the next month, but he said he'll never forget how his family's needs were met by those anonymous donors."

Sometimes learning to save money on groceries can help not only you but also others at the same time. That's what happened to Kelli Ruiz from New Mexico. She writes:

I was skeptical about whether Ellie's money-saving plan would work for me before I attended a live seminar. I wasn't sure the coupons and savings tools would be for things we needed. I prayed about it and felt like it could be a very effective way for me to save my family money, so I decided to give it a try. The month before I started couponing, I paid $542.83 for groceries; the month after I only paid $281.76! I've even given away seven bags of groceries and toiletries and still have an abundance of items—more than I've ever been able to keep in my pantry before!

In eight weeks I've saved $588.72, which enabled us to afford health insurance for the first time. I have a health problem that could eventually be critical, and now I have the means to afford the testing and treatments.

We learned of an interesting side note on Kelli's experience. After she got insurance, she fell and broke her leg severely—with medical bills totaling more than $45,000. The fact that they had health insurance saved them from a major financial crisis!

Good Getter

But how does it feel to be on the receiving end? Miel Pridemore from the Southwest knows a bit about that. She writes that her husband was waiting to get approval to go back into the air force. He worked a few odd jobs to make ends meet while they waited, but money was getting tighter and tighter as days turned into weeks and then months of waiting for red tape.

One day a friend brought her ten bags of groceries, but Miel had a hard time receiving the bounty—until the friend told her about the idea of getting now and giving later. Miel might be the one who needed the gift at this point, but at a point down the road, she would be on the giving end of the circle.

"Now," Miel wrote, "I'm giving away bags of baby food to the local shelter while I feed my family on half of what we used to spend. Who would have thought I would be able to give away so many groceries while my husband was out of work? I'm thankful for the friend who shared with me so I could share with others!"

Meals

There's a difference between donating food and donating meals. When you invite someone into your home, or take a meal to them, or even buy them a meal, you are giving that person the gift of sustenance and life. When my husband travels, he always tries to pick up the tabs of soldiers or military members standing in the Starbucks line or eating in the same restaurant as he is. If it's impossible to do it anonymously, then he just smiles and says, "It's a tangible way of thanking you for your service." He doesn't mention that he has twenty-five years in the military or anything about himself— he just keeps the focus on them.

That's what Charlene Hollaway, of Aberdeen, South Dakota, does when gifting meals. For her, giving a meal was the entry point for being able to give so much more. She keeps the focus on others. Charlene wrote in with this great story:

> Today I was returning telephone calls. One of the calls was from a member family in our homeschool group, Connie. She told me about the hardship another family was experiencing: the husband was working two jobs; the wife worked in the evenings and home-schooled during the day. And still they were without regular meals and other needs. Connie asked if we might be able to contribute a meal. I was immediately thankful for having learned your tips to save in the grocery store. Of course I would take a meal.... But had I not been reading your book, I would not have been prepared in my heart to take groceries, clothes for the children, toiletries, laundry supplies, etc. It just so happened that we had cleaned out closets this week and had the clothes ready, and their children just so happen to be similar in ages to many of our children. It also just so happened (hmm...there must be some coincidence here?) that I haven't done my shopping yet this week—so even though I don't have a large surplus to choose from, I can shop with her family in mind as well as my own.

Gifts (Re-Gifting)

So what do you do when you get three copies of *Living Rich for Less* for your birthday and Mother's Day? Well, rather than selling them to a used bookstore, you could gift them to someone else! It makes gift getting so much better when you begin to think of getting and then giving those gifts. Perhaps you wouldn't ordinarily give the postal worker or school bus driver a gift "just because." But when you get four bath baskets for Christmas, you can hang on to some of those to re-gift at a later time. It saves you money because you don't have to buy the item, but it also allows you to give when and where you might not ordinarily give. Michael Malin, from Schuylerville, New York, discovered the glory of re-gifting when his wife was pregnant.

A year ago I heard you on the radio and loved your comments. It was extremely timely. My wife and I had decided we wanted her to stay home with our youngest son, and we had been stretching our resources to the max. One of your tips was how you encouraged pregnant moms to have input in the showers they are given by friends, family, and community. Thanks to all your inspiration and advice, we ended up with one of the baby showers being a "diaper shower," where people brought bags of diapers. We had very limited financial resources but always had plenty of diapers. Then we heard about a family down the street, who was out of work due to the local layoffs at a factory, and had a newborn. We took some of our supply of diapers, which were a gift to us, and gifted them to this family. You should have seen the looks on their faces—they very much needed those! The precious gift to our family that you gave us was the challenge to give back to others. Take care, Michael

Cars

Tax laws have changed in recent years regarding the donation of vehicles to churches, charities, and nonprofit organizations. Currently you get the full value the charity gets when they sell it, not the retail value of the vehicle at donation time (as before 2005). For a complete and up-to-date list of how you can get the full benefit of your donation, go to Cars4causes.net if you live in California. For all other states, go to Donate-car-for-charity.com, which is sponsored by FCF, the Family Care Foundation, which provides worldwide emergency relief, assists in feeding and clothing third-world children, and contributes to education and even helps inner-city kids through computer literacy programs.

This true-life story comes from the Kays in Alamogordo, New Mexico (yes, that's us):

> As I mentioned, we've been able to give away several cars through-
> out our married life. I suppose the most dramatic and financially
> stretching donation happened about seven years ago. The five
> youngest kids were all living at home, and we occupied every square
> inch of our cherry red Suburban when we drove anywhere. We
> loved that vehicle because it had a television, was customized, and
> everyone in our small town knew it belonged to us! As in, "Oh
> look, the Kays are at Wal-Mart again!"
>
> We volunteered regularly as a family at a local homeless shelter.
> The older boys helped Bob paint, roof, and clean the facility. The
> younger boys and Bethany helped me weekly as we gathered food
> donations and took them to Kris and Ben King, the founders of the
> House of Prayer Mission (Alamohop.com). We saw our donations
> of money, time, things, and talents put directly into the lives of
> these people, and we saw it change the lives of many as they got off

the streets, found good jobs, and moved into their own apartments. It was and is the real deal.

But the shelter was lacking one major thing—a vehicle that would serve two purposes: (1) take the clients forty miles up the road to the nearest Social Security Administration so they could be registered and get work and (2) to ride the rails. Kris, Ben, and other volunteers would drive up and down the rough side roads and desert area alongside the railroad tracks, looking for homeless camps. They needed a truck that could handle the beating. We didn't know this at the time, but they had prayed specifically for a Suburban and posted this little note in a special place at the mission—much like putting a prayer in the Western Wall in Jerusalem. It was their prayer wall.

One day, while Bob was working at the mission, he felt a sudden urge to give them our Suburban. Crazy as it sounds, I had felt the same thing days earlier, but I was too afraid to mention it to Bob because we didn't have the cash to replace our Suburban, and it was our primary vehicle. When we both disclosed our thoughts, we were still scared but chose to give the Suburban to the House of Prayer. As we were in the process of working through the logistics of this donation, a local car dealer heard of our gift and gave us an absurd deal on a much newer white Suburban—the one we drive today.

As we drove the 'Burb up to the sidewalk alongside the mission, Ben and Kris were standing there waiting. They looked as expectant as parents who were seeing their new adoptive baby for the first time. We had all the kids with us because we wanted them to know what it's like to give from the heart and from your need. Kris began to cry, telling us for the first time about the prayer in their prayer wall. "We asked for a Suburban, but we never in our wildest dreams thought we would get a customized one in such good condition."

Ben, a retired air force master sergeant, was stoic, standing tall and rigid as his wife sobbed. Then his eyes settled on the tires—they were brand-new heavy-duty Michelins. One of the logistics Bob had insisted on taking care of before the donation. Ben broke down, unable to control his emotions any longer. He later told us, "We usually get the castoffs here since we minister to what many people consider to be society's castoffs. People think their trash is good enough for the clients we serve. But what I saw today were people who said they would give their best. It made me realize that we are not the only ones giving our best—there are others who see the value in these human lives."

If someone reading this story right now suddenly felt the urge to give in the same way we gave, then it's probably about time for the House of Prayer Mission to replace that Suburban. In fact, if Chevrolet gave me one today, it would be my greatest joy to give it away.

Furniture

People usually only give furniture items away if they can't sell them in a garage sale or in a weekly trader newspaper. But all kinds of people may be waiting for your secondhand stuff, which would seem new to them and meet their needs. Susan from Georgia wrote:

A new family moved to our small town, and their kids went to school with my kids. I have two boys, and so did "Darla," and before long, the boys started to play together and became fast friends. I tried to connect with the boys' mom, but I just didn't like her. I get along with most people, but this gal was different. She just seemed like a competitive person and had to be prettier, thinner, and more talented than any other mom—things that are all highly valued in the South. I later heard through the grapevine that this family was having financial difficulties as the dad was self-employed and wasn't getting enough work to make ends meet. Darla was putting on a front to cover her embarrassment.

One of the things they needed, since they had just moved, was a bedroom set. She and her husband were actually sleeping on a mattress on the floor. We were in the process of replacing our bedroom furniture, and my husband suggested we give this family our old set. At first I was firmly against it—I didn't even like her, for goodness' sake! But listening to my husband's sincere desire to be generous softened my heart as I realized it was the right thing to do.

I don't know who was more shocked when we gave them our beautiful bedroom set—me or Darla! She knew there was no love lost between us, and she had a hard time understanding that we were actually giving them the furniture. She thanked me and wrote a nice note as well. We didn't become best friends, but I became a better friend to my better self—one that will respond to people in need.

Appliances

The best preventative maintenance you can do to extend the life of your major appliances is to make them available for others' use. For example, when Bob and I were making one of our many military moves, we had to live in a cramped apartment for three months with four kids, including a newborn. Bob had friends who lived in town, Tom and Karen Warren, and they offered to let me and the kids come to their house to use their washer and dryer while they were at work. I much preferred this to going to the Laundromat, and it was a generous act of sharing.

Your refrigerator can store food you've prepared for others. Your water heater can heat water to give a nice shower to the traveling singing group that needs host homes for the night. Your blender can make blended drinks for the neighborhood kids—instead of the Kool-Aid mom, you can be the smoothie mom. Your oven can bake a casserole for your neighbor who just had surgery. Your freezer can store frozen banana bread to be given to anyone you have the urge to treat—the paperboy, the postal worker, or the repairperson who is fixing your disposal.

Cards

I bet you never thought of sending cards as the kind of giving that qualifies as something significant. But who hasn't received a card at just the right time for just the right reason to make just the right kind of difference? In fact, Etta, an eighty-year-old grandmother, made this her primary "job" in her later years.

> I get cards at the dollar store, at garage sales, and on clearance. In fact, ever since I started doing this, I've even had people donate their old cards to me. I make a point of writing notes to everyone in my world, including friends, family, and even the military stationed around the world. I've written to prisoners and their families and to my former neighbors and employers. It's a passion for me and it seems to give me a purpose. It's a way of giving that I can afford. I only have to buy the cards and stamps and donate my time. I don't always get a note or card in return, but that's not why I do it. When I do hear back from people who have gotten my cards, it is positive and affirming. I know that I may not always be healthy enough to continue giving cards, but as long as I can, I'm going to do it. It's my way.

Talents and Passion

Jeanette Cram has two passions: cooking and America. She's also a certifiable crumb, and the people who work with her are dubbed "crumbs" as well. There's one thing crumbs have in common—they're good cookie bakers!

You may have seen Jeanette and her crumbs on the *The Martha Stewart Show* or read about their exploits in *Good Housekeeping*. But the first place to look for Jeanette is in her kitchen. She's known around the world as the "cookie lady" and has been baking homemade goodies for soldiers on the front line since the Gulf War in 1990, when a letter from a soldier read by then-president George Bush gave her the idea. Some 130,000 cookies later, Jeanette is still preheating the oven and measuring flour. When I asked her why she has given so much time to American troops, she laughed and said, "Sometimes I get tired thinking about how big we've become—but I know it's worth it."

Everyday people like Jeanette Cram are making a huge difference in the lives of people around the world by giving of their talents, and so can you.

Sometimes your talents can even make the difference between loneliness and a feeling of community among others who are hurting, with secrets you cannot possibly know. Trust that inner voice when it tells you to give of your talent. Meet Robin from Seattle, Washington:

> I've always enjoyed floral arranging and decided to make a pretty vase of roses to put on my desk at work. I knew a lady in the office down the hall who was going through a divorce, and on a complete whim I decided to give her the flowers. Her face lit up when I delivered the roses and she started to get misty-eyed. Through tears she smiled and gulped back a sob. "I've lost of lot of friends through this divorce—my husband's sister, his mom, and those who felt they had to choose. These flowers will remind me that I will

always have the chance to make new friends." That day I felt that my passion for flowers was really destined to bring hope to the life of someone else. I'm glad I worked up the nerve to follow up on that impulse.

Sometimes your talent may be something as unique as the ability to think outside the box. This kind of talent enabled a military wife named Jessica to reach out to her community in Korea:

> I've always been a value shopper who likes to give. Back in the U.S., I can usually give openly and freely. But I couldn't always give openly when we were stationed in Korea. I'd watch a little four-year-old boy wearing only a shirt eat from my trash can every morning. I had heard that Koreans were a proud people and wouldn't eat food if you made sandwiches and set them by the trash cans—they would know you were giving them the food. So every payday we'd buy extra loaves of bread, and my three-year-old and five-year-old would help me make peanut butter and jelly sandwiches. We'd smush them and tear them apart so they would look like rejects. Then we put them back in the bread bag and tied the top. We'd dump coffee grounds to make it look like it was trash and put it in the back alleyway. As we secretly watched from the bedroom window, we saw the little boy scream in delight to his mama (they lived in a tent up the alleyway) that he had found food.

Time

In the United States, about 55 percent of American adults (close to 84 million people) give their time during the year. When we were in the military, the Family Support Center would present a check to the base commander that equaled in dollars the amount of volunteer time. It was always a huge

Twenty Priceless Free Gifts

Fix broken fences by mending a quarrel.

Seek out a friend you haven't seen in a while or who has been forgotten.

Hug someone and whisper, "I love you so."

Forgive an enemy, or at the very least pray for him or her.

Be patient with an angry person.

Express gratitude to someone in your world.

Make a child smile.

Find the time to keep a promise.

Make or bake something for someone else—anonymously.

Speak kindly to a stranger, and tell him or her a joke.

Enter into another's sorrows, and cut the pain in half.

Smile. Laugh a little. Laugh a lot.

Take a walk with a friend.

Kneel down and pet a dog.

Lessen your expectations of others.

Apologize if you were wrong.

Turn off the television and talk.

Pray for someone who helped you when you were hurting.

Give a soft answer even though you feel strongly otherwise.

Encourage an older person.

check because military families, like most Americans, like to give time. If we were to present a check to the president of the United States on behalf of America, it would be $239 billion.

If you'll recall, the total dollar amount donated by Americans annually is $260 billion. That means we're volunteering almost as much time as we are giving money. When we ask, "Who has time?" the answer is, "Others do. Why not you?"

You may not have millions to donate, but you do have the same amount of time our friends Oprah, Donald, Julia, and George have—twenty-four hours. Our time is one of the most valuable commodities today, and it's a great equalizer. Why not look at donating your time to a nonprofit organization? You could plug into a group at your church that takes food and clothing to Mexico or serves the local community in a wide variety of ways. You might want to donate a couple of hours per month at a local food pantry or soup kitchen. It could be a great way to spend time with other family members if you do it together.

Our family spends time gathering food and clothing donations for our local homeless shelter and delivers the donations in person. You might get hooked and decide you want to make an even greater time commitment and coach a soccer team, become a Big Sister or Big Brother, or volunteer in a scouting program. If you're still stumped as to what you can do, go to Volunteer.gov to get more ideas.

By the way, your kids can get involved in giving time to others around the world as well. Approach a classroom teacher, Scout leader, or after-school club about the idea of sponsoring a different nonprofit organization each month. In English class the children can write letters; in art they can draw pictures; and in Scouts they can put together care packages. When a child experiences the joy of giving time in community with others, it can teach lessons in altruism and create an orientation toward giving that will last a lifetime.

If kids are putting together care packages, they'll invest time in fund-raising, gathering donations, and organizing the packs. Some of the care packages mentioned below can be given to local homeless shelters, women's crisis centers, or even overseas military personnel (be sure to get instructions for shipment before sending care packages overseas so that all regulations are followed):

- **Toiletry Pack.** Include a sample or travel-size shaving cream, disposable razors, wet wipes, deodorant, toothpaste, toothbrush, floss, cotton swabs, shampoo, lotion, bug repellent, foot powder, and socks.
- **Food Pack.** This could include a presweetened drink mix, jerky, granola bars, power bars, bag of candy (nonchocolate), gum, canned soup, canned fruit, fruit snacks, cool snack, nuts, and trail mix.
- **Smart Pack.** Include books of all kinds, crossword puzzles, stationery, stamps, phone cards, online gift certificates, and fact books.

Encouraging Words

When my husband, Bob, flew the F-117A fighter and was on long military deployments, he spent many days away from family and friends. "There were constant struggles and opportunities to compromise moral character," he says. It was and is a constant struggle for soldiers, or anyone who is far away from home, to stay faithful to core values. This is true for firefighters who are out fighting the California wildfires, for prisoners, and even for expatriates working on foreign soil.

Giving these groups the gift of encouraging words can become the difference between success and insanity. The following is just one way some groups have worked to give the gift of encouraging words. You combine the written gift with a physical gift or reminder of that "wish." You can be creative and put together these wishes and mail the items to an adopted service member or to any of the people we've mentioned who need a good word:

- I Wish for You…the Courage to Laugh with Friends (a funny card, humor book, or family anecdote).
- I Wish for You…the Courage to Redeem Beauty for Ashes (send something lovely created out of something unusual).
- I Wish for You…the Courage to Choose Peace and Tranquillity (include a CD with a note about why your family likes that particular music).
- I Wish for You…the Courage to Cherish Memories (a personalized family photo).
- I Wish for You…the Courage to Keep in Touch (a phone card).
- I Wish for You…the Courage to Be Wise (a favorite book).
- I Wish for You…the Courage to Be Cool and Fresh (mints).

In the last chapter, we talked about whether you would consider giving. If you can answer yes, then write down three areas where you would like to start to give your money, assets, time, or talents. Write the date by which you plan to start your giving, and leave a space for when you've achieved this goal. On the next page are five examples to get you started.

Giving 'Tudes

How did you feel when you filled out your chart? Did you enjoy the process and feel challenged to give just a little bit more? Or did you ignore the chart, dismiss it as smarmy, and maybe even have an attitude about it? If you had an attitude, then realize that you are very likely to pass on that negative attitude about giving things, time, and talent to others in your world—especially if you have kids.

When our oldest son, Daniel, was thirteen, he often acted his shoe size. One day I heard him stomping up the stairs, emphasizing each step with a

Organization	Money/Asset	Time/Talent	Start Date	Completion Date
Example: World Vision	$25		Began May 1	Ongoing
Example: Homeless Shelter		Pass out towels	Tues June 15 1–3 p.m.	December 15 (six-month commitment)
Example: Salvation Army	Kids' toys, adult clothes		Truck P/U for July 8	Picked up and receipted July 8
Example: Senior Center (take kids to visit)		Gifts you give for free: hugs, smiles, jokes	Once a month starting in two months	TBA
My mom		Mend a fence	Sometime this year	TBA
Bus driver, postal worker, grocery clerk, kids' teachers		Find out birthdates and pre-address cards	Before birthday	On birthday

loud thud of his size thirteen shoe. "Work, work, work, that's all I do!" he grumbled. You would have thought I'd asked him to re-landscape with the pile of rock in our side yard waiting to be moved. He slammed a door as he began his job.

I had made the horrible mistake of asking him to empty the trash cans, something that was bound to get me turned in to the authorities.

We've taught our five school-aged children to do what we ask, but they have to do it with a good attitude. Do they always comply? No. But we keep trying because we know that a good attitude about work will one day enhance our kids' ability to provide for their families. But sometimes their work ethic needs a little tweaking. The same thing applies to our "giving ethic"—we need to be sure to give with the right 'tude.

Henry David Thoreau said, "A man is rich in proportion to the number

of things he can afford to let alone." We can afford to let alone the following typical thirteen-year-old attitudes about giving money, time, things,
and talents:

- I don't wanna, but I gotta.
- If I gotta, then I don't gotta like it!
- If I don't like it, I don't have to pretend I do!
- If I don't like it, then everyone else around me is gonna know it!
- If I do it with my attitude, then maybe I won't gotta do it again!
- If I don't wanna do it, then it's all about me—because it *really is* all
  about me!
- If I gotta be miserable, then everyone has gotta be miserable!
- But if I gotta do it anyway, and I got this 'tude, then why do I feel
  better when I get ridda the 'tude?

We can teach our kids to give their gifts without the 'tude or to forget
the gift altogether. If the reason you're doing "the big give" is so you can look
good in the shower, then give it up. Don't do it. The people you are serving
can see right through your charlatan efforts and condescending attitude. If
you give with the wrong attitude, it's as if you never gave at all—there's no
value, no true worth, no lasting remembrance of your so-called giving. Yes,
other people can still be helped, and that part has value. But any benefit to
you personally is swallowed up in the 'tude. There is a balance.

Right Attitudes Follow Right Actions

Sure, the basic idea exists that once you start to give, whether you're 100
percent there in your attitude or not, it is still worth the effort. There is
truth in that statement. But the difference lies in the core values involved
in the gift.

Let's look at a hypothetical situation involving a model and a mom.
The model throws her cell phone at her personal assistant, and the court

mandates that she give community service in order to stay out of jail. On the other side of the coin is the mom who has to rush through her service to the community because the puppy tore up her family photo album, and she's now late picking the kids up from school and in a grumpy mood.

The model is "giving" or she goes to jail. The mom is also giving with a bit of a 'tude because she's maxed out, and that stupid puppy has been chewing up everything in sight for the last four months. For the mom rushing about, she'll still feel good after she's given her gift of time or talent even though she's having a bad day. So give whether you start out with 100 percent of the right 'tude or not, and see if it corrects itself in the process. But if you're the model-turned-trash-hauler, just call it a get-out-of-jail-free card, and buy replacement insurance on those cell phones you like to throw.

How Do We Diss the 'Tude?

So how do we stop cringing when our spouse gives away another five bags of groceries? How do we get the courage to sign up to read to a group of preschoolers at the library when the thought of it makes us want to run out and get a root canal instead? One way to get the right attitude is to evaluate your motives. If your spouse is giving away clothes and food because he or she is really helping someone else out, then *we* are the ones with the wrong motives. If we feel pressured to read to those squirmy, wormy library tots because the PTA has to provide the volunteer for the week—even though it's clearly not your forte—then don't volunteer and don't feel guilty. Just guilt your girlfriend into doing it instead! Maybe doing volunteer computer entries at the library is more your style—no problem.

It might be that giving is a new concept for you. It's not good, not bad, just different—something you have to get used to before you can warm up to the entire giving mentality. A very good way to diss the 'tude is to start in your world with gifts you can give for free. In our Cha Ching Factor in this chapter, you'll find a list of these value gifts. They help you tap into your giving nature in ways that are not as threatening. Pick two from this list that are within your comfort zone, and begin to practice them this week. You'll find freedom from the negative 'tude in no time.

Living Rich Questions

Are you ready to make a commitment to give what you can and start where you are?

Did you fill in the giving chart to create a plan for donating things, talents, time, and 'tudes?

Are you willing to diss certain 'tudes and follow the Cha Ching Factor in order to give away the priceless for free?

3

Giving Green

Eco-Friendly Savings for Energy, the Environment, and Eggplant

Though old in years, I am but a young gardener.
THOMAS JEFFERSON

I hate eggplant. Always have. Always will.

My earliest recollection of this vegetable was when it appeared on my dinner plate when I was seven. I can still remember the slimy chunks looking like bits of squid with little seeds all over—no doubt the remnants of tentacles. I was convinced this eggplant stuff *had* to be an invertebrate, like the ones we'd studied in Mrs. Brewer's second grade class earlier that day. But I was afraid to ask.

My mother interrupted my thoughts, bringing me back to the dinner table with an announcement: "You have to eat at least half your eggplant, Ellie. It came from Abuela's garden, and it's good for you."

I looked at Abuela, the feisty Spanish-born woman who was barely five feet tall but was said to have wrestled a bull in the arena in Spain—and won. She was scary. As I sat there trying to decide between compliance and rebellion, she gave me her evil eye, daring me to discredit her glorious produce. Of all the vegetables in Abuela's expansive garden, we had to draw the eggplant card at this meal, fresh on the heels of squid day at school? This former *matadoress* had a green thumb that wouldn't quit, and much to my chagrin I discovered she had grown what seemed like three acres of eggplant.

I slowly took a bite of the dreaded dish and quickly washed it down with a gulp of milk. Pretending to chew, I proceeded to eat exactly one-half of the eggplant "pill style." Holding my breath helped. After each bite, I'd smile dutifully at Abuela in an effort to avert the Spanish curse I was sure she could put on me.

This proved to be a critical mistake.

Abuela smiled back and said, "*¿Quieres más, niña?*"

I couldn't believe her question. *Did I want more?*

Before I could say, "Not on your *vida*, Grandma," Abuela smiled and gave me another large helping of the stuff.

Until my adult years, I didn't truly appreciate what a green gardener my Abuela was and how much she helped our environment with her eco-friendly style of living. She used to make her own mulch from grass clippings and actually collected horse manure from stables on the outskirts of our Texas town. I thought it was totally gross at the time, but it was great for the environment. Plus she saved our family money by growing our own fruits and vegetables.

Now, before you think I'm going to suggest that you follow a horse around to gather free fertilizer, please realize that there are a lot of ways that you can do both—save money and save the environment by going green. And you don't have to follow *all* of Abuela's methods either. But you're the one risking the evil eye.

These days it's more important than ever to consider our environment and the way we get our goods and services. If Mr. and Ms. America do their part in their region of the world, it's better for all of us. I used to think that "green" people were kind of fringe and that going green meant I'd have to chain myself to a tree to stop a shopping center developer from cutting it down. But then I began to research the topic and discovered it's not about the fringe; it's about facts. The fact is, when we use less energy, we save money and resources. When I can get by with less water, I pay less on my bill and leave enough for others. It's a wonderful way to help our bottom line while helping the environment, and that is what this chapter is all about.

Here are a few ways to help keep costs down for all kinds of sustainable areas, including gardening, energy, water, household products, and more. All you have to do is make some simple changes that help you save money and live better and help our environment at the same time.

Green Gardening

If you choose to repurpose a section of your lawn for a garden, you'll find that it's really quite easy to have a green mind-set along with your green thumb by incorporating some natural ideas that promote sustainable gardening. On the section of the yard that is not a garden, you could leave the grass clippings on your lawn to return up to 50 percent of the required nutrients back into the soil. An added benefit is no clippings to bag. Another part of being a sustainable gardener is to use increasing amounts of compost or natural fertilizers such as seaweed and kelp, which will encourage plants to grow at a natural rate and also have the added benefit of keeping pests away. If you plant your garden in closely packed hexagonal shapes, you'll find that you use less water and help eliminate weeds.

By choosing hardy plants that are well adjusted to your climate, you'll be able to feed birds and attract other types of wildlife as well. During the times when your garden is not producing fruits and vegetables, you might want to consider planting alfalfa, oats, clover, or other grains. These will naturally replenish the soil, which means you'll have a higher yield next season.

Even if you don't garden, the plants you choose can be eco-friendly. For example, Langeveld Bulb Company introduced an "eco" pot last year. The natural, biodegradable pot is made of bamboo fiber and coconut, eliminating plastic that would go to landfills.

Eco Ideas for Those with No Place to Plant!

Container Gardening

You don't need an outdoor area, and you don't have to have a green thumb to grow a few vegetables in the space you have allotted. Even if you live in a college dorm or an apartment, it doesn't take much to plant some green beans or grow a tomato plant.

Basically, with some ingenuity and a little know-how, you can grow plants in window boxes, barrels and tubs, urns, or even pots and hanging baskets. Spots that are currently barren brick or wood can be turned into a miniature garden. This means you can turn a terrace, rooftop, or other unusual spot into an area to grow fresh produce.

If you read the instructions on the seed package or the directions that come with young plants from a nursery, you can determine which containers will work best for each kind of plant. Tell your nursery specialist that you are trying container gardening, and they will direct you to the plant suited for your space and sunlight availability.

- *Advantages of container gardening.* One main plus is that containers can be moved to take advantage of sunlight—most gardens need at least six hours of sunlight each day. You might want to consider keeping your containers on a movable cart for this reason.
- *Grow any vegetable.* Almost any vegetable can be grown in this way, but there are some varieties that have been developed specifically for containers and are marked as such at the nursery.
- *Use inexpensive containers.* There's no reason to buy expensive planters when garage sale or flea market finds can make the best

containers. Bushel baskets, apple boxes (fixed with wooden slats to prevent leaking), or five-gallon buckets obtained free from a health-food store or bakery make great containers. Be creative! Don't worry about a little rust or some chipped paint on an antique container; these things will add personality and texture to your garden. Just remember that each container should be large enough to hold at least six to ten inches of soil.

- *Drainage.* Container gardens need a lot more drainage than regular gardens because of the nature of the small system. You could drill holes on the sides near the base of your container every three inches, in pairs one above the other. If you already have drainage holes in the bottom, then set your container on wooden blocks off the ground. The bottom of the container should have drainage material such as tiny gravel, and this material should be deeper than the side drainage holes, or at least a half-inch deep from the bottom drainage holes.

- *Watering.* Be sure to soak the soil rather than the foliage, and water early in the morning or late in the day to avoid evaporation. Regularly water each plant according to the seed packet or nursery plant instructions.

Saving Energy

The latest report from the 2008 Consumer Expenditure Survey indicates that energy costs have risen 16.6 percent, which means the average American family will pay more than $3,600 for utilities this year. Here are some simple ways to reduce energy usage and save money:

- **Time of use**—Electricity is a big expense in the summer, and some states are offering a special discount for those who are willing to restrict their use during certain times of the day. It can be as simple as raising an air conditioning setting during the day and running your swimming pool pump at night. Check with your power company for details.

- **Energy survey**—Most utility companies also offer a free energy survey. Some regions will send out a surveyor while others offer the service via an online evaluation form. Since this is tailor-made for your home and utility usage, it's also the very best way to target specific areas that could save energy and money. Go to your utility companies' Web sites for more info.

- **CFL bulbs**—Installing CFL (compact fluorescent lamp) bulbs is one of the easiest ways to start making an impact on your energy bills. Not only will you save money and energy, but you'll also contribute to a cleaner environment by reducing fossil fuel usage. Modern CFL bulbs offer the following features and benefits:
    - Use 75 percent less energy, saving you money (energystar.gov/index.cfm?fuseaction=cal.showPledge)
    - Save more than $59 in energy costs over the life of the bulb
    - Last up to ten times longer
    - Operate at cooler temps, increasing indoor comfort
    - Produce the same attractive light as incandescent bulbs
    - Instantly start up and do not flicker or hum
    - Available in different sizes and shapes to fit in almost any fixture

- **CFL recycling**—CFL bulbs contain a trace amount of mercury, an essential element that allows them to be so efficient. This amount is extremely small, and although the mercury in just one CFL bulb does not pose a hazard to you or the environment, millions of CFLs are currently being used in households and businesses. It's important that we all make an effort to keep large concentrations of fluorescent lighting out of landfills by taking them to a local Household Hazardous Waste facility. Check out epa.gov/bulbrecycling, and click on the section for your state. Also, many IKEA stores across the country provide light bulb recycling services.

- **Energy Star–rated products**—If you want to save up to 25 percent in energy costs, then begin to look for the Energy Star rating on everything from hair dryers to small appliances and especially on larger appliances such as refrigerators. If your local store does not carry the Energy Star–rated product you want, don't let that stop you from buying green.

More Ideas for Saving Energy

The less energy we use, the less of a drain we put on our power sources, which helps everyone in the long run. An energy survey (as mentioned earlier) will direct you to the following ways to save money:

- Check your windows and doors for air leaks. Use the appropriate tape to seal leaks.
- Clean heating and cooling system filters regularly, and maintain heating and air conditioning units.
- Attic insulation should be at least six inches deep; proper amounts will save 10 percent on heating and cooling.
- Keep thermostats set at moderate comfort—68 to 70 degrees in winter and 74 to 78 degrees in summer. This can save as much as 40 to 50 percent in hot climates and 12 percent in cooler climates.
- Lower the heating and cooling systems when your home is vacant for more than eight hours.
- Use a clock-operated thermostat.

- Have your local power company perform a free energy survey. Ask them about low-cost community programs to insulate your home.
- Stop the dishwasher after the rinse cycle, or use the air dry setting. The warmth from the water cycle will dry the dishes.
- Change the vacuum cleaner bag to improve efficiency. It saves electric energy—and human energy too.
- Use your main oven for large food items. Bake as many dishes at once as possible.
- Use slow cookers and pressure cookers instead of the oven.
- Clean dust from refrigerator and freezer coils.
- Consider the EnergyGuide label on a new appliance before you purchase it.
- Consider installing storm windows and doors.

Saving Money on Water

- Buy Energy Star–rated dishwashers and water heaters.
- Set water heater to a moderate setting of around 120 degrees Fahrenheit. This keeps the water hot enough to wash clothes but cool enough to keep from badly scalding little hands.
- Wrap the water heater with an insulation kit.
- Buy a water-restricted showerhead to give plenty of water and little waste.
- Periodically drain the water heater from the bottom to remove sediment and allow for more efficient operation.
- Use your dishwasher, clothes washer, and dryer only when full to save water and electricity.
- Use cold water for your laundry. Laundry detergents on the market today will clean your lightly soiled clothing easily without hot water.

Quick Tips to Save on the Energy Bill
and Build Relationships

- Use blankets for warmth at night, or snuggle with your beloved.
- Turn off the TV. Play games with your children.
- Turn off your computer and printer when they're not in use. Instead, read a parenting book.
- Ask your teenager to help you close the damper on the fireplace when not in use, and then take him out for a Frappuccino.
- Wear a sweater in winter and shorts in the summer, and let your children help swap out seasonal clothing in order to teach them organizational skills—sell or give away outgrown clothing.
- Wear 100 percent cotton (or high cotton content) fabrics in the hot months, and walk the dogs earlier in the day.
- Keep the lint filter clean in your dryer, and teach your teens how to do laundry (a life skill they'll thank you for much later in life).
- Use the "manual dryer" outside: a clothesline. Buy extra clothespins, and have your elementary-age kids make puppets for a show.
- If you're not using something, turn it off. And every time you turn off a light switch or appliance, give yourself a hug.

- Try using less laundry detergent. Depending upon the water hardness in your area, you might need only half the amount you're currently using. The same applies to your dishwasher.
- Use the partial-load water level adjustment on your clothes washer to customize the water to your current need.

- Fix leaky toilets and faucets, especially hot water faucets. One leaky faucet wastes more than 1,300 gallons a year.
- Take a shower instead of a bath. This can save as much as 50 percent of the total hot water used in your home.
- If you're going to be away from your home for more than three days, turn off the water heater.
- Coordinate baths to conserve hot water. It takes 10 percent of the hot water in the tank to heat the lines to the bathroom. If you run the herd in and out of the shower and bath in the same hour, you'll save money.
- Read your utility bills each month, and check the meters for accuracy.
- Water your lawn in the early morning hours and only once a week (if possible).
- Fill a quart-size plastic milk or juice bottle with water. Put it in your toilet tank. This fills up space, and you use less water every time you flush.

Eco-Friendly Support Systems

Bags
In an effort to reduce the use of plastic and paper bags, most stores now offer a 99-cent reusable alternative. Buy these bags, and store them in your car trunk to use over and over again. Some stores will offer a rebate for using your own bags, while other stores are beginning to charge you for their disposable plastic grocery bags.

Organic Tags
Almost everything from hair dryers (Energy Star ratings) to clothing (organically grown fibers) is getting in on the eco-friendly act. It's not just

about food anymore. Look for these indications on a variety of products to support the eco-friendly ones.

Organic Food Products

More and more families are purchasing fair trade, where special considerations are made for social and environmental issues, including fair payment for services associated with that trade. There's also an increase in organic goods produced through natural and sustainable practices, including minimal use of insecticides and other harmful chemicals. There are cheaper ways to get more value for your dollar in these green areas.

- **Spot the rip off.** Look for products marked "certified organic" to make sure you're getting what you pay for. In the produce section, grocers are required to stock organic produce in a separate section so that water runoff from misting machines won't contaminate organic items with pesticide residue.

- **Organic sections.** Just because a product is in the organic section of the store doesn't mean it's organic. Don't be misled, for example, by the "all natural yogurt" in the organic section of the dairy case. Unless it's marked "certified organic," it probably isn't.

- **Web coupons.** I've noticed a huge increase in the number of coupons for organic products in recent years. Conduct a product name search on the Web to find these valuable coupons, including the following brands: Annie's Homegrown, Earthbound Farm, Health Valley, Organic Valley, Stonyfield Farm, and Muir's.

- **Shop discount stores.** Wal-Mart and Sam's Club have an entire new line of organics, and those sections are expanding all the time. Ask a sales associate where the organic products are located because sometimes they can be difficult to find.

Take the Quiz!

If you want to find out how eco-friendly you are, then go to Elliekay.com to take our expanded eco quiz for free! Here is the short version.

How many products do you purchase weekly that are specified as eco-friendly? (Some examples of the hundreds of available products include organic coffee, milk, CDs, baby products, home furnishings, apparel, and even eco-friendly garden mulch.)

a) 10 or more items   c) 3 to 5 items
b) 6 to 9 items   d) 2 items or less

How often do you bring your own reusable bags when shopping?

a) Every time I shop; it's a new habit.
b) Frequently; I'm trying to get into the habit.
c) Occasionally, when I think about it!
d) Never; I just don't think about it.

How many Energy Star–rated appliances do you own?

a) 3 or more
b) 2
c) 1
d) I have no idea what you're talking about (or none)

How many CFL bulbs do you use in your home?

a) 8 or more   c) 1 to 3
b) 4 to 7   d) none

How often have you purchased from "site to store"? (This is where you have products shipped from a Web site directly to a local store.)

a) 3 or more   c) 1
b) 2   d) never

From the scoring section of the Eco Quiz, you will be able to determine your results. Here is the point system:

A answers: 4 points each
B answers: 3 points each
C answers: 2 points each
D answers: 1 point each

Thrifty Taylor

If you scored between 16 and 20 points, well done. You're extremely eco-friendly. You are not only saving money by shopping smart, but you are also all about saving the environment by buying responsibly. You likely bring your own bags, buy organic, and really try to do your part to keep our planet green.

Low-Cost Logan

If you scored between 11 and 15 points, good job. You're quite eco-friendly! You are doing a good job using your green dollars in a green way! There is an awareness level on your part of what it takes to save energy, fuel, and money by making key choices that help you and your world. You can go a bit further in this area by learning to shop more organically and looking for Energy Star ratings on products.

Moderate Morgan

If you scored between 6 and 10, nice work. You're somewhat eco-friendly. You have learned to recycle and conserve in some areas, but you are probably still learning what it means to buy green. You want to help but are still figuring out how to make it work for you and your family. It's great that you have the will to help—now you just need to find the way that works best for you!

Extravagant Emerson

If you scored 5 or less, you need an eco-buddy! It might be that you've never really considered the environment or buying eco-friendly products that can help our green earth. But did you know that using a CFL bulb versus a standard light bulb will save $59 in energy costs over the life of the bulb? Sometimes saving money and saving energy go hand in hand. Why not make a few eco-friendly choices today? You could start as simply as taking reusable bags or replacing a few light bulbs. It's good for you, and it's good for our environment!

- **Buy generic.** One of the really cool things about the interest in organics is the natural continuation into store brands. Look for generic brands (which go on sale too), and save even more.
- **Food co-ops** are great sources of discounts on organic products. To find a local co-op, go to Coopdirectory.org or Localharvest.org/food-coops.
- **The food mile.** In the grocery industry there is a term known as the "food mile," which indicates how many miles food has to travel to end up in your local store. The shorter the food mile, the less expensive the product. Buy items with the shortest food mile.
- **Buy produce in season.** Oftentimes the shortest food mile means buying produce in season. By eating (and freezing or canning) your food in season, you can save money today and tomorrow.
- **Compare online grocers.** Some of the best organic grocers online might have lower prices for staples you need. Go to Sunorganic .com, Diamondorganics.com, Urbanorganic.com, or Doortodoor organics.com.
- **Go to the farm!** By going to an organic farm in your part of the world, you can save even more and buy the freshest organics possible. For a complete list, go to Localharvest.org/organic-farms.

Living Rich Questions

How many CFL bulbs do you have in your house?

What are three ways to save green (from the dozens mentioned) that you can implement this week? Think of one more eco-friendly tip that has not been mentioned, and e-mail it to Ellie today at tips@elliekay.com.

Part 2

Saving 10 Percent

The safest dollar you ever make is the one you put away

Let's say I was given one hundred Hershey's Kisses. Dark chocolate. For medicinal purposes. If I put one aside and then got all kissy-faced with the other ninety-nine, not only would I be as sick as Diane Sawyer on a media ride with the Thunderbird aerial demonstration team, but I'd also represent America's current savings-to-debt ratio. Now, if I got to go on a ride with the T-Birds (for research), I'd give up my cookies in a heartbeat just for the sheer thrill of it. Unfortunately, too many Americans find the thrill that debt can buy more compelling than the security that savings can solidify.

The average American saves $392 per year, and yet we collectively owe more than $2.5 trillion in consumer debt. The main reason we save so little and have so much debt is because we haven't learned the dichotomy of true safety. Most of us want a savings safety net, but at the same time we find that net restrictive. With the lure of easy credit and the appeal of the new and shiny, we become easy prey, cutting holes in our own safety net—tumbling into the dark hole of deep debt and an uncertain future. Instead of staying put and leaving our money in a safe place, we take matters into our own hands and find ourselves in extreme danger.

It's a vicious cycle among families I work with—we help them get out of debt and into a good savings plan…then life comes along and bumps them off the program. Sometimes a job loss or divorce gets in the way of saving and investing. Other times it could be huge medical bills or unexpected repairs on their home or car. But most of the time, in the vast majority of people I see, it's just plain materialism that cuts holes in their financial safety nets.

We're not comfortable driving an old (paid for) car or wearing last year's styles. We want a cool car seat for the new baby (the deluxe model—it's just a little more), or we want to take our family on a nice (i.e., expensive) vacation to build family memories. This cycle goes on and on—with a little debt here, a little too much spending there. You could fill out your own laundry list of "why" you can't adequately save or invest. But once again, you don't want to remain average. You want to unleash the Mr. and Ms. America within, superheroes who break the mold.

This section shows how to rise above the American norm in terms of saving and investing. You'll learn shortcuts to saving and what the best plans are for your unique needs. Maybe you have a military retirement, have inherited a house, or your kids are candidates for scholarships. This will change your investing strategy, but invest you will.

Before you can really get going and build up some speed toward your savings goals, you'll need to take care of the "d" word—*debt.* There are relatively painless ways to get a good start on that goal. Before long you'll discover how intimately intertwined the areas of debt, saving, and credit scores are and how cool it is when these areas synergize to create a positive cash flow for your future (and your kids or grandkids). Speaking of kids, I'll also show you how our family is putting all the kids through college absolutely debt free. You will see how we reversed our downward spiral and how you can experience the thrill of an upward spiral for you and those you love.

Getting financially fit is also about the journey. Yes, it's about goals, but you'll never even begin to get there if you fail to find contentment and peace in the process. You could end up a rich, restless, discontented curmudgeon if you don't learn lasting lessons along the journey. To that end, I've dedicated a portion of this section to a solid financial plan. One that is not so restrictive that you want to bang your head against the refrigerator (and knock the fire extinguisher off the top of the fridge and onto your foot—not that it's ever happened to anyone I know or anything). A plan that will make the journey a bit more pleasant instead of one that pinches your wallet, like poor Bob gets pinched when he accidentally takes our thirteen-year-old's underwear in his gym bag instead of his own. (Disclaimer: they were put in Bob's drawer by mistake and look very similar—but they are three sizes too small, and he had to wear them anyway because there was no time to go home and get the right pair and still make the test flight at work.) No, you don't want pain in the journey.

Paying down debt, building good credit, investing like you mean it, and enjoying the plan along the way—that's what we're looking at here. I know you're going to enjoy the ride. After all, you're not just anybody, and you're certainly not average—you're Mr. and Ms. America. Aim high!

4

Investing for Idiots

Forrest Funds a Dream

> But Satan now is wiser than of yore,
> and tempts by making rich, not making poor.
> ALEXANDER POPE

I was in Chicago, in a meeting at Bubba Gump Shrimp Co. with my assistant for the trip, Bethany Grace. The waiter came to our table with important business issues—trivia questions from the movie *Forrest Gump*:

Name the two rock 'n' roll artists Forrest met.

Name the three presidents he met.

Name his three best friends (one female, two males).

I got all the questions right and was feeling pretty good about life, and then Bethany Grace got a call from a *USA Today* reporter. He was researching a feature cover story on ways Americans are cutting back on luxury items. I took the call outside the restaurant (did I mention Chicago was a chilly five degrees that day?) and tried to get out of the Forrest frame of mind and into "financial expert" mode. After all those fried, sautéed, coconut-ed, and breaded shrimp, it was a hard switch to make.

"So do you think the American public is headed for a recession?" the reporter asked.

"Life is like a box of chocolates. You never know what you're gonna get," I replied.

"Um…people are cutting back on things like Starbucks and Evian water. Do you think that's smart?"

I said, "My mama always said…stupid is as stupid does."

The reporter paused. "That's fascinating. Do you have any thoughts on the perceived peer pressure among people who are saving and those who are not?"

I said, "I just had fifteen Dr Peppers. I have to go…"

After about thirty minutes of this, the poor guy had to either end the interview or end his life. I guess he's still alive, and I must have managed to say something worthwhile, as the piece ran with my incredibly Forrest-like wisdom included.

After that story broke, my offices were contacted by all kinds of major media—proving that even a goofball can know a thing or two about saving money. If you follow the saving and investing tips in this chapter, you will be able to get where you want to go. You can have savings and some luxury items too—if you put it away the smart way. Just step in my shoes, and I'll take you there because "Mama says they was magic shoes. They could take me anywhere."

And that's all I have to say about that.

One of the things I love about Forrest Gump is the fact that he became a millionaire by doing what was right and following common sense. Yes, I do understand that Forrest is a fictional character. Nonetheless, I feel like Forrest is one of my people. I find myself doing idiotic things like putting the milk in the oven or paying for my food at Del Taco and driving off without my order. The word for it is *momnesia,* and as a mom of so many I have a terminal case of it. But that is the beauty of life, isn't it? You don't need the intelligence of a Bill Gates or the influence of a Warren Buffet to succeed financially. This mom of many has found great financial success and has been able to teach others how to live the rich life—despite the odds!

Forrest could get rich, and so can you! You can find the financial success that Bob and I found for our family by following the same ancient financial principles that work. Yes, they work—every time, for anybody, even if you're from Greenbow, Alabama. These principles apply to the average American who makes $48,000 per year (keep in mind that 85 percent of our population makes $100,000 or less). This chapter is for the way Mr. and Ms. America invest in order to pay the bills, get out of debt, put their kids through college, and fund their retirement.

If you spend less than you make and wisely invest the difference, you too can invest like an idiot and come out living the rich life. Here are some areas to pay attention to on the saving and investing journey.

Savings

When people ask me what they should do with some money they have to invest, I usually ask them two questions:

1. Are you out of consumer debt?
2. Do you have enough money in your regular savings account?

If you are in credit card debt, the first thing you should do with that money is pay that debt down and out. If you've got a good interest rate, you're paying 10 percent. If you're on the higher end of the interest scale, then you could be paying 23 percent or more. Very few sure investments have a solid 10 percent return these days, and fewer show upward of 23 percent! Therefore, the best place to park that money is in your checking account, where you'll use it to pay off those cards as soon as possible.

Second, it's more important to build a solid regular savings account than it is to invest in stocks and bonds. If yours is a one-income family, you should try to have six months' worth of living expenses in your savings. If you have dual income, you should have a minimum of three months' living expenses in your savings account. The reason is obvious—if there's only one wage earner, and he or she loses that job, no other source of income is available until one of the partners finds employment. If there are two wage earners, they'll feel the pinch if one of them is suddenly out of work, but there is still another person bringing in money. I like to use Ingdirect.com or Bankrate.com because of their higher interest rates for savings and higher yields on CDs.

As you build your savings account with 10 percent of your net income, you need to keep in mind that we're still talking *savings* here, not investing. A savings account not only builds a buffer for the possible loss of employment, but it allows for those unexpected expenses that arise—like a new roof, tires, braces, repairs to a broken-down car, replacing old appliances, etc. A savings account is there so you can pay cash for these items instead of financing them. It also allows the luxury of time in seeking the best buy. The secondary motive of savings is for consumable expenses such as vacations, luxury items or splurge items (however you define that), entertainment, etc. If you concentrate on saving for essential needs rather than optional wants, you'll be in a much better position to accumulate wealth and have the freedom to do some no-kidding real investing.

Start Saving Early

Look at our next table, which shows what investing $50 per month will do based on 10 percent interest compounded monthly. You'll see that the person who starts saving early and stops after eight years will yield bigger returns than the person who starts saving later *and* saves for twenty-two years. It's simple math, and it's simply astounding.

Age	Saves Early		Saves Late	
21	$600	$600	0	0
22	600	1,386	0	0
23	600	2,185	0	0
24	600	3,063	0	0
25	600	4,029	0	0
26	600	5,092	0	0
27	600	6,262	0	0
28	600	7,548	0	0
29	0	8,303	600	600
30	0	9,133	600	1,386
31	0	10,046	600	2,185
32	0	11,051	600	3,063
33	0	12,156	600	4,029
34	0	13,372	600	5,092
35	0	14,709	600	6,252
36	0	16,179	600	7,548
37	0	17,798	600	8,962
38	0	19,578	600	10,519
39	0	21,535	600	12,231
40	0	23,689	600	14,114
41	0	26,057	600	16,185
42	0	28,663	600	18,464
43	0	31,529	600	20,970
44	0	34,683	600	23,727
45	0	38,151	600	26,760
46	0	41,964	600	30,096
47	0	46,160	600	33,765
48	0	50,777	600	37,802
49	0	55,854	600	42,242
50	0	61,440	600	47,126

Investments

Once you've built your savings account by putting aside at least 10 percent a month, then it's time to look at other investments as well. Each family is different, but generally speaking I would advise you to pay down debt, build your regular savings account, fund your 401(k) and Roth or regular IRAs (for both you and your spouse), and then build college funds. Along the way, a variety of other investment options are available, including mutual funds, stocks, bonds, and college funds.

401(k)

Most of you already know that a 401(k) is an employer-sponsored savings plan that allows employees to contribute a portion of their salary to a savings plan. One of the great aspects of the 401(k) is that money directed to the plan may be partially matched by the employer. In the best-case scenario, some companies will match 100 percent up to the limit.

Even employers who are cutting back to a mere 25 percent matching funds are still an excellent deal for workers. If your 401(k) fund doesn't perform well in a bad economy, you still have the 25 percent return of the employer's match. So don't let dwindling balances in your fund keep you from investing—especially when your employer is matching those funds! In the 401(k) plan, your investment earnings (interest, dividends, and capital gains) within the plan accumulate tax free until they are withdrawn.

Employee participation in 401(k) plans could be a lot better, but it seems that the primary reason people don't contribute is because more and more major companies no longer offer the matching portion for their employees. Another reason is that the fund may perform poorly in a time of economic challenge, and people don't want to pour money into a fund that isn't yielding high returns.

Unless you're desperate and cannot contribute due to some dire finan-

IRAs "R" Us in Three Easy Steps

It's very easy to set up an IRA.

Step 1: Find a Discount Broker. If you don't already have one, we suggest you look into opening a discount brokerage account. For a complete chart that compares different brokerage firms and the fees associated with them, go to Investment Ally (see page 89). This broker should be able to handle IRAs, Roth IRAs, rollover accounts, spouse IRAs, and education IRAs.

Step 2: Open and Fund Your Account. Once you've compared discount brokers and decided which one is the best fit for your financial needs, it's time to open your account. Most brokers have an online application you can complete and can electronically transfer funds from your checking or savings account. However, some brokers require that you print out the form and mail it in with a check.

Step 3: Invest It! Once your check or electronic transfer has cleared, you're ready to start investing. That means deciding which stocks or mutual funds you want to buy or consulting your broker for his or her opinion and instructing your broker to buy the stocks or mutual funds, thereby funding the account.

cial straits, stopping contributions to a 401(k) is a bad idea. You aren't getting any younger, and each generation seems to live longer. Predictions are that it won't be uncommon for baby boomers to hit age 100. Hey, if 40 is the new 30 and 50 is the new 40, then why wouldn't 100 be the new 80? Chances are good that because of this longevity factor, you'll need more money in your retirement than any generation in history—you'll still need to eat, live, and have certain services and care. If you don't continue to participate in your 401(k)—no matter what the economy, no matter what the matching portion—you risk deteriorating your financial future in retirement.

The other reason you should keep contributing is that you would miss the tax deferral, which is a ginormous benefit. If you're in the 28 percent tax bracket and put $10,000 in the plan, it only costs you $7,300 of actual money you would take home. This means that the tax deferral alone is an instant 28 percent return on your money.

The bottom line is: Unless you're independently wealthy, have a rich uncle, or have some other options to fund your retirement, you'll need a fat 401(k). Set it up to be an automatic withdrawal from your check, and you'll never miss what you never see. Remember that pretax contributions are the fastest route to building the kind of wealth you will need for retirement.

While different kinds of 401(k) plans with various benefits and limitations are available, the purpose of this chapter is not to take the time and space needed to completely cover these details. The purpose of this section is to get you well on your way to investing, not to give an extensive course on the nuances of the 401(k) versus the Roth 401(k), or the difference between participant-directed funds or trustee-directed funds. When you change employers, you will need to roll over your 401(k) funds to either an IRA or a new 401(k) plan with your new employer. Be sure you know how long you must be employed for your employer's matching portion of the fund to be vested. It may vest immediately (meaning it is yours), or you may have to be with the company for a year or longer before the matching portion of the 401(k) will be yours to move to a new fund (via a transfer or a rollover). Or you could leave the money where it is if your old employer allows it. See the next section on IRAs for help in finding a discount broker who can help you move funds from your 401(k) to an IRA. If you're interested in learning more, I've got a deal for you. Just e-mail LivingRich@elliekay.com, and in the subject line enter "Investment Ally." Some beautiful, talented person from our staff will send you a special link for this resource. This is only available to *Living Rich* readers, and this section of the Web site is not viewable without the specific link. In our Investment Ally, you'll find greater detail on all the investment sections referenced in this chapter.

IRA

An individual retirement account (IRA) is a personal savings plan that allows you (and your spouse) to contribute up to $5,000 a year. If you're fifty or older, you can make an additional $1,000 catch-up contribution. Every dollar you invest today will work for you until you are ready to start playing in retirement. The sooner you open an IRA, the more money you'll have for your golden years. I plan on doing a lot more skydiving and rock climbing—I just don't seem to be able to schedule those into my calendar very often.

If you have earned income and are under age seventy and a half, then you can make a contribution to a traditional IRA. The only question is whether that contribution will be deductible. If it's not deductible, there are still benefits to funding your IRA annually (a detail found in Investment Ally, see above). Whether your IRA is deductible or not depends on your income tax filing status and whether you (or your spouse) participated on any day of the year in an employer's qualified retirement plan.

In general, if neither you nor your spouse participated in a 401(k) or other qualified retirement plan, your contribution will be fully deductible. For details, you can go to the Investment Ally resource I mentioned earlier in this chapter.

Roth Versus Traditional IRA

There are two basic IRA options that you should evaluate and choose between in order to continue to grow wealth through investments: the traditional IRA and the Roth IRA. Choose a Roth IRA if you can do without the tax break right now (or if you don't qualify for a tax-deductible IRA). It's a more flexible instrument because:

- It allows you to withdraw your contributions at any time, penalty- and tax-free.
- You do not have to take mandatory distributions at age seventy and a half.

Choose a traditional IRA if you need the tax deduction right now, if you have not contributed to a 401(k) or SEP, or if you anticipate paying taxes at a significantly lower rate in retirement.

I fund our IRAs once a year, but everyone has until tax day in April to make a contribution to an IRA for the previous year—it's not like you have to make it by December 31. This is good because it gives you time to gather the money to put into your IRA. I recommend that you figure out how much you'll contribute for the year (let's say $2,000 for you and $2,000 for your spouse); divide it by 52 weeks ($38.46 per person); and allocate that amount as an automatic withdrawal to go to the account you've set aside for funding your IRA. When it's automatic and made before you get your check, it's a lot easier to prioritize it. The goal is to work toward fully funding IRAs for both you and your spouse (a weekly allotment of $76.92). When tax day rolls around, you'll fund your IRA and start saving for next year's contribution.

Entrepreneurs: Creating Wealth from Home

As you've probably noticed, I really love the idea of creating small businesses and seeing them succeed. It's one of the things that sets Mr. and Ms.

America apart from the pencil-necked geeks in the office—they have their own ideas on how to start a home-based business. One of the ways to fund your investments is to create wealth from home. This small section is in the investment chapters because (1) home-based businesses can help fund investments, and (2) specific tax-favored investment vehicles are available to small-business owners. Establishing your own home-based business is a wonderful way to pursue your passions—whether you work full-time for someone else now, stay home full-time with the kids, or are going to school for a new career. Loads of people out there are making it work after leaving a previous profession to pursue the independence and challenge of their own business.

It's great when some of these passions and interests end up making money for the family coffers. While we won't go into great detail on all the nuances of setting up a business, a good place to start is with the following ideas:

- Ask your librarian to help research your chosen field.
- Look up books, magazines, and newspaper articles.
- Talk to other people who have done what you'd like to do, and follow them around.
- Join an industry organization.
- Subscribe to industry publications.

The first part of research is to determine passions and interests. It's important to consider taking a personal skills and interests assessment. One such free assessment is called Personality I.D., a new, unique, and validated interactive personality assessment tool that allows the respondent to view him- or herself and others from a fresh, new perspective. Its primary purpose is to help the individual identify and understand his or her unique personality. By understanding personality and how it causes an individual to operate, it might be easier to decide what kind of home business would best suit a particular kind of personality. These assessments may also be available at a local library, community center, college, or small business administration (SBA) center.

Picking the right resources; asking questions about any multilevel marketing business; and assessing inventory requirements, start-up costs, and tax liability are all essential to a successful home business. For even more detail dedicated to this topic, just e-mail LivingRich@elliekay.com and put "Home-Based Business" in the subject line. We'll send you enough information to make your eyes glaze over!

SEPs

One of the greatest benefits I enjoy from my own small business is when it started to make money and I was able to set up a Simplified-Employment Pension plan where I could contribute up to 25 percent of my compensation. I set up my SEP without a CPA's help, but you might feel more comfortable having a professional set up one for your business. It was that easy—there were no complicated IRS forms to file or administration fees to set it up. The forms were fairly simple and painless. But my CPA tells me how much to fund it with each year when he prepares my taxes. If you're a sole proprietor, it's a good move since you file on yourself only, and it will give you a fully portable retirement fund that you control. Remember that you don't need a certain number of employees or amount of income each year to file. The woman who sells Premier Designs jewelry can put away 25 percent of her profits in this tax-favored account as easily as the man who owns the jewelry store in your local mall! It's a gem of a deal.

Question: If your employer has a 401(k) plan, are you maxing out your benefit? If you are self-employed or one family member has a home-based business, do you contribute to a SEP fund? If not, map out a plan to start funding these within the next three months—starting where you are and giving what you can.

A Dollar a Day

Albert Einstein once called compounding interest the eighth wonder of the world. Look at the following chart showing what investing a dollar a day will yield. You could give up your daily candy bar and soda to help *more* than your waistline. Higher interest rates tend to be more speculative, so beware of the risks involved. You'll see it's worth the effort to save your dollar a day.

One Dollar a Day
Cumulative Return

Years	Total Invested	5 percent	10 percent	15 percent	20 percent
10	$3,600	$4,658	$6,145	$8,257	$11,283
20	7,200	12,331	22,781	44,917	93,290
30	10,800	24,968	67,815	207,698	689,335
40	14,400	45,781	189,722	930,482	5,021,546
50	18,000	80,060	519,732	4,139,793	36,509,163

College Savings the Kay Way

Man, I love my kids! Truly. When they aren't trying to spend me into oblivion, they're making me rich. When they aren't driving me absolutely stark raving bonkers, they're thrilling me down to my very tippy toes. It's a constant juggling act, this parenting thing. We have to teach them to manage money and look to their own futures, but we also want to give them room to step out on their own and succeed or fail while they're still under our roof.

When people ask me how we are putting this many kids through college debt free, the answer is multifold.

First, we trained our children from a young age that going to school, doing their homework, and getting good grades is their primary job. By teaching them a good work ethic, we are laying the groundwork for scholarships and more.

Second, we send them to schools that we can afford or where they get the best scholarship offers to cover the most expenses.

Third, we've saved a modest amount of college money to help them pay their room and board and partial tuition in some cases.

Last, but certainly not least, we require that they work part-time in the summer or during the school year (through a work-study program or a regular job) in order to do their part in paying for college. By implementing these four disciplines, each of our children is set to graduate debt free. These days, at any given time we have three kids in college at once. Yes, I think I deserve a medal or at least a ride in a Thunderbird jet. Among the three that are going to college now, we have more than a half million in scholarships, and if the last two stay true to their goals, our kids will have garnered over a million dollars in scholarships by the time they're through with school.

First Things First

In any discussion of college costs, it's important to keep priorities straight: You've got to leave yourself some fun money for retirement. How else can you afford the mechanical bull–riding lesson and those parasail flights (been there, done that, love it)? I've heard that space rides on the Virgin Galactic are ten million dollars—that's gonna take some time to save for as well!

I really believe that you as a parent should try to avoid borrowing on your future in order to pay for *your child's* future. After all that information earlier in this chapter about investments for retirement, why would you want to take one of your greatest investments (i.e., your home) and leverage it for college expenses? Yet millions of parents make that devastating financial choice every year. I'm talking about avoiding any college-funding plan that includes a home equity loan, a HELOC (home equity line of credit), or refinancing an existing home mortgage. These options reduce the amount of equity in your home, increasing the risk of possible foreclosure, and you incur interest charges that may cost you more if the term on the new mortgage is greater than the remaining term on the existing mortgage (for example, ten years are left on the existing mortgage and parents get a new thirty-year loan). Furthermore, if parents choose to pull out enough money in equity for four years of college all at once, they're paying interest on money that won't be needed until the upcoming sophomore, junior, and senior years. Instead, look at the following options to pay for college.

The College Mantra

When I was a young adult, got married, and began having kids (in that order), I was first exposed to the whole idea of "the college my child gets accepted to." As a mom of many who has already launched a few college-bound kiddos, I'm still hearing, "What college did so-and-so get accepted into?" The part of that question that amazes me is that the most impressive answer is also the most expensive one (Columbia, Harvard, Stanford, Yale). These schools have average four-year costs of $188,000 (Columbia); $240,000 (Harvard); $186,000 (Stanford), and $193,000 (Yale).[1]

While an average of 40 percent of the students who attend get financial aid, grants, or scholarships, those only average out to assistance of $9,600 per year. This leaves a boatload that the student and Mom/Dad owe for college. Most of this is usually in loans of some kind. So the average student graduating from some of the most prestigious colleges have student loans upwards of $100,000.

So why the question: What college did your child get accepted into?

The question should be: What college did your child get accepted into that he or she can afford?

Why do you want to leverage your future (through HELOCs or other loans) or leverage your kids' future (through massive consumer debt) when it will take many years of earning power for them to pay back those loans? One of the most common problems I hear about has to do with the burden of dual student loans in a marriage.

The new mantra should be: "I will go to the school where I can get the best education possible for the least amount of student loan debt."

One of the best things you can do for your college fund is to teach your kids a good work ethic at home and at school. Ride the homework train on them in the afternoons. Teach them that getting good grades; pursuing passions in sports, academics, and the arts; and working hard are their main jobs throughout school. And be sure to let them know that you expect them to not only get scholarships but also to participate in work-study programs, have jobs in the summer, and actually earn part of their way through school!

If you want to see how this million-dollar mantra worked for us, wait until you get to the final chapter of the book. You'll be motivated as you follow these college savings ideas when you see what our family has accomplished.

Investing in Creative Savings Methods

Before discussing traditional financial savings plans to pay for college, I want you to consider the fact that any way you pay for college that doesn't involve a cash investment is more money in the bank for you and your student. The following ideas are ways to pay for a college degree through plans that are available for those who are forward thinking and purposeful in their desire to provide a debt-free college experience. We've used several of these for our kids, and every thousand dollars we *don't* have to spend on tuition, college credits, books, or room and board is a thousand dollars that will counter the huge student loan debt that most parents assume as par for the education course.

It's an adage I've used before: a penny saved is more than a penny earned, especially when it comes to paying for college.

The 10/10/80 Rule for College

In our discussion of the first 10 percent of the 10/10/80 Rule, we saw that giving away that first 10 percent can apply to money, time, and talents. Here is where some of that giving pays off. When you've trained your child to give back to the community, don't let those good deeds go unrewarded. Organizations such as Teachforamerica.com, Peacecorps.gov, and Americorps.org all offer educational service awards to students seeking cash and a way to make a difference in the world. The best part is that unlike other scholarships and grants, these service awards won't affect any federal financial aid eligibility. Even if your student has already acquired student loans, organizations including the Army National Guard, National Health Service Corps, and the National Institutes of Health all sponsor loan forgiveness programs that turn borrowed cash into free dough in exchange for postgraduate service.

Double-Dipping: College Credit in High School

- **AP and IB.** Several of our kids have taken Advanced Placement or International Baccalaureate classes throughout their high school years. These are college level courses offered at their high school. At the end of the year, they take a test to see if they score high enough to get college credit. The cost of the test is more than offset by the value of the college credit that will be awarded to your student if they pass. It's important to note that not all colleges accept these credits, so it will be important to check with the admissions office of the college of their choice. A secondary benefit of these courses is that they can help students get into college, because having AP and IB credit makes for very good résumé fodder in college applications. It shows ambition and a good work ethic. For information regarding your state's programs, go to the National Association for College Admission Counseling, or Nacacnet.org.

- **Dual Enrollment Classes.** One of the coolest ways to pay for college is to let your local school district help pay for it while your child is still in high school. Many school districts now partner with local colleges to offer college credit for high school students who take classes at a nearby community college. Consequently, these classes count toward both the high school and college degree requirements. Thousands of kids each year graduate from high school one day and get an associate's degree the next day. Talk about a Cha Ching Factor! Be aware that these programs vary from district to district and state to state. In some cases, the dual enrollment classes take place in the high school during the regular school day. Other programs require students to attend classes on the college campus, alongside other college students.

- **Balance in All Things.** Bob and I are very careful about the fact that we want our kids to be kids and not have adult responsibilities too soon. There is, however, a balance. While we are real sticklers about homework and housework and don't allow the kids to treat us like their maids, we do understand that they are still kids and need to have fun in their childhood. Consequently, if they're enrolled in AP, IB, or college classes while in high school, we try to make sure they don't overdo it. We limit their extracurricular activities and discourage a regular part-time job so that their primary job will be to get good grades in their advanced courses. It would be self-defeating to have them take advanced or college classes only to have their overly busy schedules negate their ability to get good grades. Remember, there's no credit if they don't pass the AP or IB tests or the college course. So look closely at the curriculum before you sign your student up, establish work and study habits, set boundaries to preserve the integrity of their grades, and leave room for kids to be kids and have fun!

- **Community First, Four-Year Later.** Think of it as a half-price sale for education: Buy two years at full price; get two for half off (or more). The average community college tuition rate is 40 percent of the average tuition at four-year public colleges and 10 percent of the average tuition at four-year private institutions. If your child attends a community college for two years, you'll not only save money on tuition, you'll also save on room and board and transportation by sticking close to home. The key to getting the most value for your education dollar is to make sure these college credits are transferable and to assure they're working toward the four-year college goal.

- **Employee Discount.** My high school friend Karyn Maxwell had a dad who was a baseball coach. He worked his way up to the college level, and by the time Karyn's older sister graduated high school, he was the baseball coach at Texas Christian University. Both Karyn and her sister went there for free thanks to his employee benefits. If you or your spouse has some latitude in your career, consider working at a local college for the tuition benefits it would afford your children. Most universities offer some form of tuition remission to their full-time employees, and others extend the benefit to part-time employees as well. If you can't secure a staff position at the school of your choice, don't forget that many companies offer tuition reimbursement packages. A study conducted by the Society for Human Resource Management estimates that 67 percent of all employers offer financial assistance to employees seeking an undergraduate degree.

College Savings Plans for Every Family

Now that we've exhausted the creative alternatives to pay for college, let's take a look at some traditional methods. Saving for college is as individualized as your dreams. College aspirations vary from family to family and even from child to child. Your plan will also vary based on different factors such as your income level, the number of children you have, the amount of college savings accumulated, scholarships, federal aid availability, and the number of years before a child starts college. Here's a guide to the most popular investment tools:

- **Uniform Gifts to Minors Act (UGMA).** Parents of young children can start saving now for education but do it the tax-smart way. By investing in an UGMA in a child's name, income is taxed at the child's marginal tax bracket rather than at the parents'. The account *must* be registered in the child's name. An adult (usually a parent or grandparent) serves as custodian and is responsible for investing and managing the assets. But the child is the "beneficial owner," meaning the assets really belong to the child. At age eighteen (in most states), control of the assets must be turned over to the child (which could be a disadvantage for this plan when it comes to financial aid qualifications). All states offer UGMAs, and many have adopted the Uniform Transfers to Minors Act, or UTMA, as well. An UGMA allows children to own stocks, bonds, mutual funds, and other securities, while an UTMA allows the children to also own real estate. Under UTMA, parents can delay giving the assets to the child until age twenty-one. For example, if your beautiful bouncing three-year-old daughter has interest income of $700, the tax on that is zero. If she has income of $1,400, the next $700 is taxed at her 10 percent rate. If you're in the 28 percent bracket in 2009, the tax on the $1,400 total would be around $400. Your daughter is only paying $70, so you've just saved $330 more for her college education.

- **Series EE U.S. Savings Bonds.** If income from these bonds is used to pay for education expenses, that interest may be excluded from taxes. But this exclusion is phased out beyond certain income levels.
- **Zero Coupon Bonds.** The interest on these bonds is deferred until they mature, when it is paid in a lump sum. Parents do have to pay income tax on interest as it accrues each year the bond is held. It's often wise to "ladder" these bonds, where the bonds come to maturity in each year of the child's college career.
- **529 Plan.** This is an education savings plan operated by a state or educational institution designed to help families set aside funds for future college costs. As long as the plan satisfies a few basic requirements, the federal tax law provides special tax benefits to you, the plan participant (Section 529 of the Internal Revenue Service found at irs.gov). These plans are usually categorized as either prepaid or savings, although some have elements of both. Every state offers a 529 plan, and it's up to each state to decide what it will look like. You can go to Finaid.org to review your state plan. Educational institutions can offer a 529 prepaid plan but not a 529 savings plan (the private college Independent 529 Plan is the only institution-sponsored 529 plan thus far). Parents can invest in any state's plan, no matter where they live and regardless of what plan they choose, and their beneficiary can attend any college or university in the country. What's more, grandparents or other benefactors can contribute money to a 529 plan. However, 529 plans may crimp a child's ability to get financial aid in the future. It is important to review the state ratings for residents and nonresidents, as some are rated better than others. These plans are growing

in popularity. It is projected that a total of $175 billion to $250 billion will be invested in 10 million to 15 million accounts by the year 2010.

- **Coverdell Education Savings Accounts (ESA).** This will allow up to $2,000 of pretaxed income to be invested annually if the modified adjusted gross income is less than $95,000 as a single tax filer or $190,000 to $220,000 as a married couple filing jointly in the tax year in which the money is contributed. The $2,000 maximum contribution limit is gradually reduced if the modified adjusted gross income exceeds these limits. There are limits on how much can be invested based on income, and the funds must be spent before the child turns thirty. This education IRA will not interfere with the parents' ability to invest in a tax-deferred annuity in their own retirement account, but it will count heavily against the student when financial aid packages are calculated. Because Coverdell ESA funds can be rolled into a 529 without penalty, parents can sidestep its principal drawbacks—the age limit and the fact that the ESA counts as the child's asset, which can adversely affect his ability to receive need-based loans. Therefore, a Coverdell account may be the best single investment option for parents whose income is below $50,000. The accounts are easier and less expensive to set up than 529 plans, and people in this lower tax bracket aren't usually able to take advantage of the maximum lifetime contributions allowed under a 529, which range from $110,000 to $305,000, because they don't pay that much tax in the first place.

- **Prepaid Tuition Plans.** A 529 prepaid plan is one that is offered in individual states or educational institutions, and they are prepaid similarly to a 529 plan but are less risky. They allow parents to pay tomorrow's expenses at today's prices either by the year or

by the credit hour. The drawbacks are that even though parents can
often transfer some of these plans to other state colleges or private
institutions, those schools do not guarantee the same services and
prices. Thus college students could come up short. Contributions
to prepaid plans might also reduce a student's eligibility for financial aid on a dollar-to-dollar basis, more so than with a 529 plan. If
the child does not attend college, the contributions are refundable,
but there might be a cancellation fee and/or loss of interest earned.
It's important to compare 529 plans to find the plan that works
best for different families. You can go to Savingforcollege.com to
review the latest updates on these various plans. These plans are
best if parents (1) don't expect to qualify for financial aid, (2) are
conservative or novice investors, and (3) understand the risks.

- **Financial Aid Office.** The university's financial aid office is a
clearinghouse of information. A good aid office will not only
help students determine what loans they qualify for, but will also
steer them to participating lenders who are offering the best terms
and service. Parents can do their own assessment by visiting
Collegeboard.com's "Paying for College" Web page calculator
found at Payingforcollege.com.

- **Filling Out the FAFSA (Free Application for Student Financial
Aid) Form.** The FAFSA (found at Fafsa.ed.gov) is the first step in
applying for aid that includes: (1) need-based guaranteed loans
(Stafford loans are variable, while Perkins loans are fixed); (2)
grants—the Pell Grants and the Federal Supplemental Education
Opportunity Grant each provide a gift of up to a designated
amount per student per year; and (3) work-study. Students can
receive up to $2,000 per year, 25 percent of it matched by the par-
ticipating institution, from the federal work-study program. Some
other options that the financial aid office might offer are tuition

deals when your student is a freshman. Some schools may allow
you to lock in your student's tuition for four years if you are willing to pay more the first year. By choosing that option, some families are saving a boatload of money by the time their student is in
his or her junior and senior years because many universities raise
tuition every single year by as much as 8 percent. The only caveat
is that if the student leaves the school, you don't get a refund on
the premium you paid that first year. There are also state loans and
grants available, and the financial aid office should be able to
quickly assess the student's eligibility.

- **Scholarships.** Millions of dollars of scholarship money go
  unclaimed every year. This is free lunch money that parents or
  prospective students who are willing to do some detective work
  may find more quickly than they think. Fastweb.com has over 1.3
  million scholarships to research. Don't forget to have students
  apply for local civic organizations' and community scholarships as
  well—the high school counselor should have a list of these scholarships. The final chapter of this book will show you the results of
  our own family's personal experience with scholarships.

Living Rich Questions

Do you have three to six months of living expenses in your savings account? If not, then decide to start funding one with at least a minimum of $25 weekly from your paycheck to your savings account. Make it a goal to build up this allotment to 10 percent of your income. Map out the incremental increases, and make a note in your calendar to authorize these automatic increases with your bank.

Are you training your kids *now* on how to achieve a debt-free college experience?

Do you have a traditional IRA, Roth IRA, or other mutual fund? If not, check out our Cha Ching Factor, and plan to fund one within the next six months—starting where you are, contributing what you can.

5

Fat Tuesday

The Debt Debate

What a lot of things there are
a man can do without.

SOCRATES

When I was in the eighth grade, I was five feet eight inches tall and weighed 125 pounds. I was a petite size 6. Life was a lot easier when my problems were smaller than my waistline. I was simply too young to appreciate how good I had it. It only took five pregnancies and twenty years for me to fully appreciate my eighth-grade year!

During that time, my friend Donna (who was also petite) and I convinced ourselves that we really needed to lose five pounds. Thankfully my Spanish mom had a no-nonsense approach to life that helped me get a grip before I could even *think* of falling into the teen trap of perfect bodies and eating disorders.

It all started when Donna and I made ourselves accountable to each other to only eat nutritional foods and forgo sweets. But my *mamacita* had a plan. On Tuesday of that week, after I came home from a three-hour drill team dance practice, I was famished. My mom had whipped up my favorite chocolate cake, knowing full well that I couldn't resist the sweet indulgence. That was my fat Tuesday—I chowed on chocolate cake. I immediately asked Mom to please not tell Donna. But I knew I was in trouble when she smiled sweetly and said in her upbeat Spanish accent, "Oh Kay, chew know dat I no say nothing!"

Now you have to know that my mom has a great sense of humor and often uses her accent to make people laugh.

Later that week, my mom drove Donna and me to the mall, and much to my horror, my mom proceeded to tell Donna about my misdeed.

"Today, Doo-na, Ellie she no so good."

Donna was polite. "What did Ellie do that wasn't good, Mrs. Rawleigh?"

"Today, Ellie she eat de cho-co-laa-te cake. She sheet on her diet!"

I was mortified for more reasons than one. For starters, I wasn't too hip on Donna's knowing about my dietary indiscretions. But even worse was the embarrassment I suffered over my mother's pronunciation of *cheat*. It came out of her mouth as a combination of *sheet* and a well-known four-letter word of similar sound. Donna and I went to Young Life youth group together at school, and *no one* in our group used those kinds of words!

Donna about swallowed her tongue as she responded to my mom's announcement, "She did what, Mrs. Rawleigh?"

Mom looked in the rearview mirror at Donna in the backseat. "Leesten, Doo-na, I tell you already, she sheeted. I told her she no should sheet. But she no leesten to me!"

Later that day I pulled my mom aside. "Mom, can I talk to you a moment?"

She stopped dusting the coffee table and gave me her full attention. "Sure, what do chew want to talk about?"

I didn't know how to broach the topic, so I just blurted it out. "Well, Mom, it's about your accent."

"What ax-cent? When I *first* come to de United States of Amereeka, I have an ax-cent. But I no have no ax-cent no more!"

Despite her denial, I was a teenager on a mission. "I know, Mom. You've really lost a lot of your accent. But there are still some words that you don't pronounce correctly. And when I'm around my friends, the way you say certain words embarrasses me!"

Mom was genuinely concerned. "Well, I no embarrass you for nothing! You tell me de words and I will practice!"

I looked at her eyeball to eyeball. "Mom, earlier today you told Donna that I 'cheated' on my diet. The way you say the word *cheat* sounds like a dirty word!"

The rest of the day, as she cleaned house, she practiced her enunciation skills.

Each time she dusted a lampshade, cleaned the bathroom mirror, or wiped down a kitchen counter, I overheard her saying, "My daughter, Ellie, *shee-ited* on her diet."

Cheating On Your Debt

Whether you're talking about diets or debt, cheating in any language can get you into trouble. And when it comes to finances, many Americans have been cheating themselves every time they increase consumer debt. When Bob and I had so much debt, we were really limited in what we could do, where we could go, and whom we could help. I really hated that feeling because I was such a giver and wanted to help a lot more people than I was able to help. Even after we got out of debt, if we spent too much of our disposable income, we would find ourselves right back in the same restrictive situation. So part of the process was learning to be content while we got out of debt so we would continue to be content and free up extra money to invest. It's a constant tug of war, and if you let up, you'll end up in the pit again. So we must continually be mindful of the temptation to spend. It all began with getting rid of the fat—debt.

If you want to live rich, the first thing you need to get rid of is credit card debt. Just like the woman who uses Spanx pantyhose to shift the weight around in an attempt to look thinner, poor money managers have their own "weight shifting" techniques that appear to make the debt load seem lighter than it really is.

What are some indicators that you've been dipping into the Hershey's Kisses of excessive credit card debt? Are there warning signs that you're quickly approaching a Fat Tuesday (the most decadent day of Mardi Gras) of debauched credit card behavior that is leading to an Ash Wednesday (the day you repent of your Fat Tuesday excesses) of regret? How do you know if your debt load is getting in the way of reaching your financial dreams? Is all credit bad, or can credit be used as a tool? Let's find some answers to these common and important questions.

Fat Tuesday Warning Signs

The following are *some* (but not all) of the indicators that your use of credit cards is a barrier to living rich:

- The use of credit card cash advances to pay for living expenses
- Using and depending on overtime to meet the month's expenses
- A steadily increasing revolving balance on credit cards
- Using credit to buy things that you used to pay for in cash, such as groceries, gasoline, and clothing (that you do not pay off when the card bill arrives)
- Using overdraft protection on your checking account to pay monthly bills
- Using savings to pay bills

- Using one credit card to pay another
- "Floating" the bills: delaying one bill in order to pay another over-due bill
- Using another loan or an extension on a loan to service your debt
- Using a cosigner on a note
- Paying only the minimum amount due on charge accounts
- A FICO (Fair Isaac) score of less than 600. (This is the credit score that lenders often use to evaluate creditworthiness—see the chapter on FICOs later in the book.)

If you answered yes to two or more of the Fat Tuesday warning signs, you could be on the way to serious debt problems.

The Living R.I.C.H. Principle

If after reviewing your Fat Tuesday you realize you need some help, what should you do? Begin with the idea of living R.I.C.H., and you're four steps from debt to financial freedom.

As I mentioned before, Bob and I had $40,000 worth of consumer debt when we got married. He took a $15,000 pay cut to fly jets in the air force. One-third of our income was going to child support, and then we had five children in seven years and eleven moves in thirteen years. That's a total of seven children that need to be provided for in every way. It wasn't feasible for me to work outside the home, so stretching a dollar and paying down debt became my new job, and I was up for the challenge. It would be an adventure.

But that can-do attitude didn't change the fact that we were in a world of trouble. It was during that time that we discovered the hidden treasure in our lives. It was an asset that was worth more than a million dollars, an asset that gave us hope. This hope would be our redemption; financial woes would be subdued, and we would get our lives back, only better. The first step was to get out of debt while trying to juggle and pay the bills. You see, we had eight of those twelve warning signs mentioned in Fat Tuesday. Some well-meaning people recommended that we file for bankruptcy, but we decided to develop and live by the R.I.C.H. Principle instead. Here is the acronym that changed our lives:

R for Redemption: Claim financial redemption, and admit you have a problem. To be redeemed means to be set free from some kind of bondage—of body, soul, mind, or spirit. In our case, our debt was holding us captive; we had a poor-mouth mentality, as we constantly used every kind of excuse to be in debt and stay in debt. We were trapped. We decided to break free.

We knew our debt was devastating enough to rob us of our future, our marriage, our family, and our kids' futures. Money problems are stated as the number-one reason for divorce, so we needed to admit we had a problem and recognize that our finances needed to be redeemed. We were bondservants to our lenders. We wanted to be set free in order to live the rich life we were meant to live.

It's probably not a huge shocker when I say that we are people of faith. We believe in God—along with 88 percent of Americans. But faith without action would be ineffective. We knew that the only way our finances could be redeemed was by taking the first step to acknowledge the fact that we had a problem and needed a solution.

I for Instruction: Submit yourself to wise instruction. Throughout this book you'll learn how debt is a cruel taskmaster, and you'll be instructed on how to regain control of your money. Bob and I began to follow principles of good stewardship—the idea that all our resources and wealth were things we had a responsibility to manage well. What we discovered is that these principles work no matter what your religious beliefs might be. The instruction we received helped me develop the 10/10/80

Rule. For example, if you give away the first 10 percent, you'll always have enough for your family. If you save 10 percent, you'll have money for the future, and if you spend the last 80 percent wisely, you'll be able to pay your bills, put your kids through college, pay off your debts, and live rich.

If, and only if, you follow wise instruction.

C for Commitment: Absolutely commit to put any unexpected income toward debt repayment. We knew that we had to commit to pay down our debt, so we verbally committed to put every unexpected bit of money that came into our household toward our debt. We didn't waffle. We were steadfast, and all of heaven knew it by our actions. Something incredible happened to that $40,000 of debt when we committed to do everything to get rid of it. The checks began to arrive in the mail.

The first check was from Grandma Laudeman—$50 for my birthday. It may seem like a little amount, and who could've begrudged me for spending it on something nice for me? But I remembered our commitment and the principle that "he who is faithful in the little things will also be faithful in much." So I put it toward a Visa balance. Then we got a $300 check from USAA, our insurance company. It was a dividend rebate on our premiums. It went to American Express. The next refund check came from a GI Bill bonus that we didn't know Bob qualified for, and it was almost $3,000. Although we were tempted to spend "just a little," we remembered our commitment, and it was used to finish paying off the Visa and American Express cards. The final boon was when I won $20,000 on *The Price Is Right*. Although it wasn't in cash, we were still able to give away one of the prizes—a cooking range valued at $3,500. It went to a homeless shelter, and the travel trailer we won was sold and the money put toward our debt load.

Within two and a half years, we not only paid all our monthly bills and the child support and kept the kids clothed and fed—we paid *all* of the

$40,000 in debt. Without a commitment to pay down the debt, we wouldn't have been able to find the financial freedom we so desired.

When you make the commitment to paying down your debt, you will also need to decide which debts to pay off first. If you have eight cards with balances, then pay the one with the least amount first in order to create synergy and momentum. The idea of having only seven left and then six and then five will give you that good feeling of making progress. If you have two debt balances that are the same amount, the wise move is to pay the one with the higher interest rate first. With commitment and hope, you'll find you are making significant progress toward living rich.

H for Hope: Befriend a companion named Hope. No matter what stands in the way of your financial freedom, no matter what obstacles arise, no matter who tries to stop you—have hope for the future. It's easier said than done. Horrible financial and emotional issues arose for us due to Bob's divorce, and we almost lost hope several times. Then we realized who was in control—and it wasn't the credit card companies or the ex-spouse or the courts or the problems. We had committed our finances to the principles of good stewardship—the 10/10/80 Rule—and we had hope that those principles would work for us and our family. That's not to say it wasn't hard—it was downright despairing at times. But when Despair knocked on our front door, asking entry into our home, we slammed it soundly in his face and walked with Hope instead. We didn't always know how it would work out, but we knew we would be all right—thanks to Hope.

If you're serious about living the R.I.C.H. life, take a look at the following letter of commitment. Accountability is one of the most effective tools that Mr. and Ms. America, superheroes of today and tomorrow, have in their arsenal. This letter provides the grounding you need to get rich in a healthy and lasting way.

R.I.C.H. Letter of Commitment

We, the undersigned, being of a somewhat sound mind and ever increasing body, do hereby commit to live a R.I.C.H. life. We hereby acknowledge, under only a moderate amount of duress, that we have a specific financial problem in the area of _____, and we will seek to find financial redemption for this problem. We also agree to abide by wise instruction—by hanging out with wise guys (and we don't mean the Sopranos) when it comes to money matters, realizing that we have often made foolish decisions that have not been a benefit to our bottom line or our way of life. Furthermore, we agree to commit to implementing this instruction in our lives and using all our resources to get out of debt, address our other financial problems, and stop the madness that has kept us from living the rich life we desire. Finally, we choose to close the door on Despair or any other negative spirit that seeks to overtake our decisions, minds, and actions. We choose, instead, to embrace Hope and realize that if a crazy woman like Ellie Kay can have all those kids and all that debt and find financial freedom, then we can too!

    Signed,

    _____ and _____

    Dated _____

    Witness _____

Hidden Credit Card Costs: Problems and Solutions

Did you sign the commitment letter above? Think about it—there really is power in writing something down on paper. There's even more power when you invite a trusted friend to be the witness and hold you accountable, just like Donna and I, silly little eighth graders, decided to make ourselves accountable for our so-called diet. You too can invite a financial counselor, a friend who is good with money, a clergyperson, or a wise family member to witness your decision to break free of the debt game once and for all.

Once you've dealt with the philosophical idea of R.I.C.H. living, it is time to embrace the practical. But where should you put your energy and efforts? Part of the process is found in understanding the credit card system.

Just as my mom "worked" on trying to say *cheat* correctly and had little success, many consumers work on getting their credit card debt under control but repeatedly find barriers to their success. One of the primary hindrances to gaining control over debt comes from the credit card industry itself. Even though the competition for customers has never been fiercer, some credit card companies are finding ways to make these services cost cool consumers like you more money than ever.

If you're not careful, you may become prey to legal methods that some of these companies use to charge more for using their cards—especially if they feel you're becoming a higher risk during a wayward economy. It's not that credit card companies are big, bad, scary ogres who are out to get you. It's simply that credit card delinquency rates are rising to 30 percent in the present economy, and bankruptcy filings are also near all-time high levels. Lenders are taking a huge hit and are looking for ways to recoup their losses.

That's why it's important to choose your credit-card provider very carefully. Here are some debt factors used by credit card companies that you can avoid in order to reach your goal of living rich.

Waking the Dead

If you have an old, unpaid credit card lurking in your closet, beware when you decide to open a new card. According to Liz Pulliam Weston, a writer for *MSN Money,* John Witters of Davie, Florida, was delighted to get a low-rate offer from Capital One a while back. After all, his credit wasn't the greatest, thanks in part to about $1,500 worth of credit-card bills he failed to pay to his previous credit-card company. Imagine his surprise when that

$1,500 debt showed up on his new credit card. Witters insists he didn't know he was "reaffirming" or agreeing to pay the old debt, when he signed up for the new card. [The new lender] is equally insistent that the deal was spelled out in the solicitation he received.[1]

Some lenders are buying previous debts from other creditors and trying to entice borrowers to repay the debt with a new credit card. This is a legal action as long as these terms are disclosed to the client, but sometimes the information is in the fine print of the document the client signs.

There are two steps you can take to avoid waking the dead:

1. **Pay old debts.** The most obvious way to stay a step ahead of a spotty credit history is to make good on old debts. Even if your debt has been written off and no creditors are breathing down your neck, you could contact the previous creditor and make arrangements to pay down that debt. Not only could it help improve your credit score, it will be an old debt that is settled and can no longer come back to haunt you.

2. **Read the fine print.** Remember that just because a new bank or different credit card company is offering a card, you could still potentially owe an old debt if it has been bought by a new company. If you don't understand the terms, then call the potential creditor and ask for clarification before you sign on the bottom line. The old adage remains true: If it sounds too good to be true, then it is probably is.

What If the Dead Awakes Anyway?

I recently saw *Young Frankenstein* on Broadway with my Naval Academy son, Philip, who was in New York City with me while on leave. We had a blast, and I remembered the first time I saw a Frankenstein movie as a kid. Just when the monster came to life and opened his eyes, my dad came up behind me on the couch and shouted, "Blubluablua! Blubluablua! Blua!"

That was *not* fun for me at all.

Just like Frankenstein's monster, not all collection agencies operate within the guidelines of the Fair Credit Reporting Act (FCRA), and they dig up that corpse and bring it back to life. The FCRA states that a bad debt is dropped off a credit record after the seven-year statute of limitations has been met. Some credit agencies have even been known to purchase the bad debts, report them with different dates, and give new life to old debts for another seven years. Unlike the previous practices we listed, this one is flat-out illegal and a scam according to the Federal Trade Commission (FTC).

There are two steps you can take if you find yourself with a Young Frankenstein on your hands:

1. **Contest the debt.** If the customer protests, he or she can request that the collection agency investigate and correct the illegal entry. This should be your first line of defense.

2. **Decide on a next step.** If the collection agency refuses to make the necessary investigations and corrections, then let them know that your next step will be to contact the National Association of Consumer Advocates (Naca.net) for adequate recourse. Often-times the threat of possible litigation is enough to encourage these collection agencies to complete their due diligence and do their part. At this site is a list of possible legal representation from attorneys who specialize in these kinds of disputes. You will be able to find the legal means to minimize the negative impact of the unfair reporting on your record. It's also important to con-tinue to monitor your credit and identity histories by subscribing to a monthly service such as Creditexpert.com.

FeeFee

We didn't have pets growing up, but our neighbors did. Mrs. Kooperman used to go outside with her dog on hot Texas afternoons and take a sunbath.

She just lay on her lounge, and little Fifi, her poodle, lay in the shade underneath. Mrs. Kooperman only got freckles and never got tan. I thought it was
the strangest sight and kept watching for the day all the freckles would run
out of room and be joined together into a no-kidding tan.

Credit card companies also own a dog named FeeFee, and their little
poodle knows a lot of tricks. This old dog is learning new tricks. The
amount of money collected in late fees has risen four times as much as pre-
viously charged in less than a decade. Believe it or not, lenders collected
$26 billion in an assortment of fees in one year according to the GFOA
(Government Finance Officers Association).[2]

Not only has there been an outbreak of payment delinquency among
consumers, the penalties have also become much, much greater. Here are
some facts to consider:

- **Late fees.** The average late fee in the summer of 1994 was $11.97.
  This rose last year to the current average of $30.04 according to
  Cardtrak.com. Don't think that just because you have a platinum
  card you'll pay lower fees. According to Cardweb.com, while Platinum Visa and MasterCard have generally come to signify the
  issuers' highest credit limits and lowest pricing, a platinum offer
  may also include some of the highest fees for making a late payment, going over the credit limit, or taking a cash advance.
  According to a sampling of platinum solicitations dispatched in
  June and captured by Cardweb's new "CardWatch" service, platinum late payment fees are 31 percent higher than the industry
  average.

- **Over-limit fees.** More bad news. The fee for going over your limit
  rose in the same period from an average of $12.57 to $28.00.

- **Cash advance fees.** The fee for a cash advance used be a $2 mini-
  mum and $10 maximum with a 2 percent interest fee. Today, fees
  are between $10 and $50 and charge higher interest rates than

your normal card rate, oftentimes between 20 to 25 percent inter-est. The interest is charged as soon as the clock starts running on those advances. Also be aware that those checks you get in the mail from your credit card companies are just cash advances in this cat-egory. Those are two reasons you should never use a credit card for a cash advance.

- **Grace period.** It is easier to make a late payment than ever before because some lenders have reduced grace periods (the time you have to pay your bill before it is considered late) from thirty days in 1990 to an average grace period of twenty-one days in 2008. Two out of three people paid at least one late fee last year, and most paid three. Also be aware that a credit card company may suddenly change its grace period on an account you've held for many years. For example, they could change it from twenty-five days to only twenty-one days; however, they must give notification of the change before it goes into effect.
- **Card fees.** This is the annual fee your lender charges to allow you to keep their card. While the introductory fee may be waived or minimal, the subsequent fees could be quite high—even double in some cases. It pays to know what you're paying on your annual fee.

Training FeeFee, the Wonder Dog

If you're smart, you can resist this old dog's new tricks by retraining your-self to pay attention to credit card payments and transactions. Five specific ways to counteract the problems were mentioned in the previous section. Here are six more:

1. **Act immediately.** When your credit card bill arrives, pay the minimum payment right away—especially if you have a twenty-one-day billing cycle. You can always send a larger payment at the end of the month—and hopefully you will because it's important

to start paying down your debt as soon as possible. Better yet,
follow the next step to automate your payment.

2. **Automate it.** Whether you normally carry a balance or not,
you can set up an automated payment with your banking institution by going to your credit card's online site. The payment
would be for a few dollars more than your estimated minimum
payment each month. This way you can make sure you won't
have a late fee.

3. **Ask!** If you are charged a late fee and do not have a history of late
charges or other delinquencies, call the lender and ask them to
remove the late fee. Many will do this if you take the time to
ask—especially if you fit the "good customer" criteria.

4. **Avoid cash.** Use your debit card to get cash instead of your credit
card. If you get into the habit of getting cash on your credit card,
you not only pay additional fees, but you could go into greater
debt and have little or nothing to show for it.

5. **Annual fee reduction.** About two and a half months before your
card is set to renew, or if you receive a notice that your lender is
replacing your old card with a new and improved version, call the
credit card company and ask what the annual fee will be. If you
are a good customer and have a solid history with this company,
ask them to waive the annual fee in order to keep you as a happy
customer.

6. **Attention, please!** Pay attention to the notices you get in the
mail. Your creditor is required to notify you of all changes in
advance. This includes the adjustment in grace periods, interest
rates, and card provider changes. In the fine print brochure you
receive, you are allowed to decline the new terms and pay off your
account under the old terms, but you would also have to give up
the card and not make new charges.

Do You Know Your Credit Card Habits? They Do!

I don't want you to get panicky over the idea that Big Brother is watching you, but…Big Brother is watching you. Lenders track your charges, payments, and spending habits. Part of this is good because if you suddenly start charging lingerie in France and swimming suits in Germany and you've never charged anything outside your state before, this Big Brother practice can alert them to possible fraud.

But like so many things that can be good but may have a negative underbelly, you need to be aware of your own habits because they could work against you. This awareness can save you money on interest and fees.

Areas to Guard

- **New accounts.** Lenders consistently review credit reports. If you are opening too many charge accounts (even for furniture or a 0 percent APR automobile loan), you could take a hit with an increased APR on your credit card.
- **Late payments.** Not only will you pay a substantial late fee, as we just discussed, but you could also pay a higher rate if you're late with as few as two payments. Other card providers could follow suit as well.
- **Revolving balance.** It's important that you don't charge more than 50 percent of the available credit on the card. For example, if you have a card with a limit of $8,000, in order to keep the best rates, you should carry no more than $4,000 as a revolving balance on that card.
- **Maxing out cards.** If you are maxing out your credit limit, it could send a message to lenders that you are getting into debt overload with the potential of not having the means to pay your

bills. Consequently, you could get hit with a higher rate because you are becoming a greater risk to the lender.

- **Paying the minimums.** In the past, lenders seemed to encourage borrowers to carry a balance and to pay only the minimum payment due on the debt. They even reinforced this concept by making the minimum payment only 1 percent of the total debt instead of the standard 2.5 to 3 percent. But things have changed in recent years. Those min-paying customers are beginning to be viewed as potential risks. Can they pay all their debts? Are they paying the minimums because they are living month to month with no additional funds yet still have available credit? Not only does min-paying mean accruing tons of interest, it could indicate that you are an at-risk customer who may be more likely to default on a loan. Some minimum-paying customers are now having their rates raised to as much as 20+ percent simply because they don't attempt to pay down the balance. This habit also lowers your FICO scores.

- **FICO.** Your credit rating, or FICO score, affects your rate. If you don't know your credit rating, you can be sure your lender does! Customers with a lower credit rating (generally 600 or less, depending upon the lender) will pay a higher APR. I talk more about FICO scores later in the book—what they are, why they're important, and what you can do to improve yours.

Turn Big Brother into a Gentle Giant

You don't have to be afraid of Big Brother or be at his mercy. Knowledge is power, and now that you are learning what creditors look for in establishing rates and fees, you can make this knowledge work to your advantage. Here are some specific things you can start doing today to lower your APR or to make sure it isn't suddenly raised:

- **Pay on time.** Paying all your bills on time will help you keep your rates down. We've already discussed a couple of ways to make sure you pay your bills on time.

- **Pay more.** Even if you pay only $5 more than your minimum payment, you are *still* technically paying down your debt, and this will be reflected on your credit history.

- **New applications.** Be aware that every account you open, whether a store account (to get that 15 percent discount offer), furniture charge account (to get the "12 months same as cash!" deal), or appliance sales account (who can pass up the free extended warranty?) will hit you on your credit rating. Keep these applications to a minimum. Or better yet, turn them down.

- **Don't max out.** Don't consistently max your credit card limit unless you can pay it off at the end of the month. Better to divide the debt among a couple of cards than to keep maxing out a single card. Even if you can pay off your card at the end of the month, another reason to be mindful of your credit card limit is that creditors are now giving consumers a hit if they charge more than 10 percent of the available credit in any given month—even if they pay off the balance at the end of each month. Ask them to raise your credit limit, or shift the monthly charges onto two or more cards to make sure you meet this requirement.

- **Don't min out.** Some points are worth reinforcing: Pay more than your minimum for better credit scores. If you pay only the minimum on a $2,000 balance, it will take you eighteen years to pay off the debt, and you will have paid a total $4,600 with interest! But if you pay only $25 more than the minimum on a $5,000 balance, it would take sixteen years off the time it takes to pay the debt *plus* save you $3,000 in interest.

- **Credit report.** Check your credit report at least three times a year. You can do it for free and even get a copy of your report by going to Annualcreditreport.com. Each of the three major credit-reporting agencies is required by law to give you a copy once a year. You can order these at the aforementioned site for free— stagger your requests to once every four months and you'll have a good pulse on possible fraud and any errors that arise.

Dispute errors (more on that later), check for fraud (possible identity theft), and close department store cards you don't use. Or contact any of the three credit reporting agencies directly at:

- Equifax: (800) 685-1111 or Equifax.com.
- Experian (formerly TRW): (888) 397-3742 or Experian.com.
- TransUnion: (800) 888-4213 or Transunion.com.

Transfer Trouble

You probably get several offers a month from lenders who will give you a fantastic APR if you transfer your existing debt load to their card. Have you ever been tempted to take them up on their offer? Have you ever *done* it? I've worked with people who gave in to the quick fix once—before they knew it, they were transfer addicts! Here are the traps to be aware of in the "transfer temptation":

- **Bait and switch.** Sometimes a lender will make a great initial offer for a fantastic rate in order to get you to transfer your balances to its card. However, unless you have a good credit score, you may not even get the great rate! Even some prequalified accounts don't get the lower APR. Instead you might get approved for the card but at a higher rate.
- **Fees.** Some consumers don't realize there could be substantial fees for balance transfers. Most lenders charge at least 3 percent for

balance transfers, which could eliminate the benefit of the lower interest rate.

- **Longevity.** Part of a good credit score is determined by how long you've kept a card and been a good customer. The longer you've held a card (and paid well), the greater your credit limit tends to be, and an unused credit balance looks good on your credit rating. If you cancel a card you've had ten years in order to get the lower APR on a new card, you may lose the benefit of longevity with the first credit card company, thereby allowing your credit rating to take a hit.

- **Higher rates for newbies.** Although you may or may not get a great rate on balance transfers, your new purchases might still be subject to the higher rate. In fact, if the new card's primary rates are higher for you, then you could end up paying more in the long run on your new charges if you are a regular charge customer. The reason for this is that all the payments you make will first go toward the lower rate charges while the higher rates continue to accumulate interest longer.

- **FICO hit.** Opening and closing multiple credit card accounts hurts your credit score. The lenders can see what you're doing— trying to float the balance and go for the best rate. In the long run, you'll likely hurt your credit score and end up paying as much (if not more) in fees and hidden higher interest rates.

Transfer help

Now that we've seen all the ways that transferring debt can get you in trouble, realize that not all transfers are a bad deal for the consumer. It is important to know how and when to make a transfer. Here are some tips that will help you make the most of these opportunities.

- **Two for one.** If you'll be using a card for balance transfers (and it meets the criteria in this section), then use it only for the lower transfer rate, and use your old, established card for new purchases. That way you're paying the best interest rate on the transfer balance and the best (or lower) interest rate on your existing card.

- **Count the cost.** If you do want to transfer a balance to a new card, get a disclosure up front of transfer fee costs and any setup fees for the card itself as well as the annual renewal fee. After you've done the math, then determine if it will be a good value to switch. A great tool to calculate these costs as well as get card descriptions and fees can be found at Bankrate.com.

- **Minimize the number of cards.** Try to keep your balances on one or two cards in order to keep up with the time constraints on introductory APRs, payment due dates, and other card details. You are more likely to make a mistake (and pay a large penalty fee for your error) while trying to keep up with too many different cards.

- **Read the fine print.** Before you apply, make sure the bait-and-switch tactic described above won't apply to the new card or to your situation. See how long you will qualify for the lower introductory APR (for the lifetime of the balance or for only a few months), and make your decision accordingly.

Let's take a mental break right now and go on a little vacation. We deserve it after delving into the nitty-gritty world of credit card debt! If you were given a free trip anywhere in the world and a credit card to use for a shopping spree, where would you go? Picture yourself on the beaches of Bora Bora having a spa treatment or in the Waterford Crystal factory in Ireland selecting that exquisite vase. Maybe you would peruse fashions in France, shop for Lladro figurines in Spain, buy a Hummel in Germany, or snarf down chocolates in Belgium. Can you picture yourself there yet?

Unfortunately, most of us don't have a free shopping spree coming on our credit card when we have the rare opportunity to travel abroad. Not only do most of us have to pay the bill, we also have to pay the fees associated with exchanging foreign currency. The exchange rates vary greatly from card to card, and you need to think strategically about which card you take on that dream vacation. Here are some facts that could help you make that decision. (May you one day have this dilemma—it means you're on your way!)

Take the Right Card on Your Dream Vacation

- Paying Abroad: Credit cards tend to be the best way to purchase items overseas—you have less risk of cash being stolen, you tend to get a better exchange rate, and you don't have to worry about re-exchanging unused foreign money on your trip home.
- Convenience and Acceptance: Credit cards are also more convenient than traveler's checks because not all businesses overseas take traveler's checks.
- Fees: The typical fee for overseas transactions on your credit card ranges from 1 to 3 percent, depending on the card. Sometimes the only way to find out what rate your card charges is by calling the credit card company and asking. Use the card with the lower transaction and conversion fees.
- Ask: When you research your card before you travel abroad, if you aren't satisfied with the transaction percentage charge, ask them to waive the regular charge or reduce it to 1 percent.

Living Rich Questions

Did you answer yes to two or more of the "Fat Tuesday" credit warning signs? If so, then purpose to take the steps necessary to get fiscally healthy.

Will you review the R.I.C.H. concept and sign the letter of commitment today?

Are you paying too much in credit card fees? What is your plan to stop?

6

Fun, Fun, Fun!

The FICO Factor

The only point in making money is you
can tell some big shot where to go.
HUMPHREY BOGART

I like to have fun. I work hard and play hard. That's what makes life an adventure. My adventure fix is usually met while I'm on a trip—I'll take a side trip to go skydiving, bull riding, or parasailing. But sometimes adventure comes to me—and it isn't always fun at the time. This was the case when I flew Southwest Airlines a few months ago on a trip to Chicago.

When I travel on Southwest, I consider it a matter of traveling life-or-death to get in the "A" boarding group. That day they called our flight, and everyone crowded around the gate, waiting to get onboard. As we stood elbow to elbow, trying not to step on anyone's toes, a short man in his fifties suddenly turned to a tall man about the same age and shouted, "Hey! What do you think you're doing? Do you want me to kick your a*#!?"

The taller man was clearly startled and said, "What are you talking about?"

Napoleonic Complex Guy replied, "You pushed me! You definitely pushed me! I'm gonna kick your a*#! Just try it again. I dare you!"

"I did not push you!" the tall man responded. He was standing about three inches from me as he asserted to the other guy, "I barely touched your bag. There are so many people here it's no wonder!"

"You did not just touch my bag. You pushed *me* and I'm going to kick your a*# into the ground. Try that again. I dare you!" Shorty was out for a fight and started to clench his fists.

Finally the taller man, in an effort to protect his manhood and apparently unable to resist a double-dog dare replied, "You and whose army? You couldn't kick my a*# in a million years!"

I looked around for a Southwest employee and noticed that the gate agent had stepped outside to check something on the plane. My pulse began to race as fast as if I were standing in the doorway of an airplane, strapped to my flight instructor, and ready to jump out. But as the wife of a fighter pilot, I've learned to remain calm in crisis.

The gate area was deathly quiet as everyone looked on in amazement while the argument escalated and the two men began to shout.

The guys were fisting up, about to come to blows.

I quickly checked off a mental crisis-assessment list as only a mom of large-footed teenage boys can do:

1. They had no guns (they've gone through security).
2. They had no knives.
3. If one of them hit me, ten men would be coming to my rescue in an instant.
4. If they fought, we would undoubtedly be delayed while they took the big babies' luggage off the plane, and I would miss my dinner meeting—the main reason I was going on this trip.
5. I'd broken up fights between my six-foot-five-inch son and my six-foot-four-inch son when they'd threatened to come to blows. I could do this.

Before I realized what I was doing, I stepped out of the sidelines and found myself right in the middle of the two men. I had to repeat myself three times before they finally heard me, even though I was only inches away.

I raised my voice: "Gentlemen!"

"Gentlemen!"

"GENTLEMEN!"

Finally, they paused in their war of words and looked at me.

"Gentlemen!" I said. "This is *not* worth it!"

Everyone in the gate area watched the scenario play out. "Gentlemen. If you continue this nonsense, not only will the authorities take you off this flight, but everyone in this gate area will be delayed because they'll have to remove your luggage from our plane."

I stared them in the eye and spoke with my best mama voice. "Not only that, but the people in this gate area are going to be very upset at your childlike behavior, and everyone will suffer because the two of you are arguing over nonsense. Whatever you're fighting over is simply not worth missing this flight!"

They didn't reply, and I keep motoring forward since I had momentum on my side. "Furthermore, you need to stop this right now and get a grip on yourselves."

The tall man stood back as if someone had just slapped him in the face and brought him to his senses.

The Mickey Rooney wannabe was undaunted. He turned his angry stare on me and looked ready to begin a tirade of wrath directed at me. But as I watched his eyes, I could tell that even though he was furious, he was processing the information I was giving him. It was true that this was a ridiculous fight. It was true that he would be kicked off the flight. Before he had a chance to fully process the information, I stuck my finger out and looked him in his beady eyes. "And you? Turn around now!"

He looked a bit dazed, then glanced around the gate area at all the people staring. Slowly, he turned back around in line.

The people in the gate area breathed a collective sigh of relief as many of them began to cheer the mama who took control of the situation.

The gate agent soon returned and we began boarding. My heart was racing as I came down from the adrenaline rush of what I'd just done.

As I boarded and looked for open seating, I felt a hand on my arm. It was the tall man.

He looked up with a face full of embarrassment and shame. "Thank you," he said quietly.

I felt compassion for the boy inside the man who felt compelled to respond to a double-dog dare.

"You're welcome. Peace. Peace to you."

I actually felt sorry for the man who was provoked into acting badly. I've been in similar situations when it comes to being under pressure and reacting badly. I'm embarrassed of the times I've snapped at the grocery store clerk when she made a mistake on the bill or when I've ripped the postman for a damaged letter. When that happens, I ask myself, *Where did that come from?* The good news is that I'm not that way all the time; the bad news is that I'm more likely to snap and make bad decisions when under pressure.

When it comes to some of the money decisions I've made, I look back and wonder how I got myself into those messes. But I remind myself that a mess is better than a disaster, so even a mess can be viewed as improvement. When it comes to credit scores, it's very easy to get yourself in a mess rather quickly, especially if you don't know what areas have a greater impact on your score. The people I've worked with who have the biggest problems with their FICO scores are those who were tricked into making bad decisions. Some of them were actually thrust, against their will, into risky financial moves due to a medical emergency or a job loss.

The FICO Score Challenge

Following are three steps to improve your FICO score immediately—are you up to the challenge?

1. **Pay a day early** rather than a day late (set up an automatic pay plan online).

2. **Pay more than your minimum** balance on each credit card (even $5 to $10 more).

3. **Pay proportionally.** Make sure your proportionality is not more than 50 percent on each card (if your card has a $6,000 limit, make sure you don't have more than $3,000 charged on it).

There you have it. Take up the challenge, and you'll be the winner at the end with an improved FICO and a better chance to recession-proof your credit score.

At other times, people get into trouble because of childish behavior, getting suckered into buying things they don't need in order to please people they don't like. They can feel dared by the commercials on screen that say they have to buy a certain car to feel happy. In the end, those dares will have their day, and the result is a credit score that takes a beating. If you've made some careless mistakes or been out of work, gone through a divorce, or had a medical trauma, this may or may not be your fault. But you can still do something to improve your credit rating (your FICO).

You may not even know what your credit rating is right now. While more than 90 percent of Americans know what a FICO *is,* only 33 percent know what their personal scores are.

Basically, your credit score is the number that is calculated from data in your credit report. These scores help lenders make fair credit decisions since FICO scores reveal facts to them that relate to your general risk. The factors involved in the rating are based purely on the numbers and not on race, religion, nationality, gender, or marital status. While some people assume that these last two factors (gender and marital status) are credit risk factors, that is a misconception.

Although some women may not have credit scores as high as their male counterparts, it usually has more to do with whether they have established credit history of their own and developed a good individual credit history rather than from joint accounts. Many women do not realize that their individual FICO score is a different number from their husband's. Each has their own rating. In the case of joint credit, the factors involved will affect both spouses, but the individual numbers are still separate.

Unfortunately, there are groups of women who haven't yet realized the importance of cultivating their own good FICO score. If they find themselves in a situation where their spouse is suddenly out of the picture (due to widowhood or divorce), they may feel the ramifications of a low FICO when they venture into the world alone. It's important for everyone—male or female, single or married—to know how to improve their FICO and use it as a tool.

I receive a lot of questions about this topic when I speak and in my in box, so let's look at some of the most common concerns:

Many aspects of your life are impacted by your FICO.
A good credit score is invaluable to every American. In a nutshell, here are the benefits of a good score:

- **Loans.** A good credit score helps you qualify for loans and get faster loan approval.

- **Interest rates.** Your FICO score oftentimes is the determining factor when it comes time for a lender to give you an interest rate. A better rating can help you get a better mortgage rate and could even make the difference between becoming a homeowner rather than a renter.

- **Promotions or jobs.** More and more employers are checking FICO scores before they take on a new hire or when considering which of their employees will get the next promotion. Why should they let you be responsible for more of their company when you cannot be responsible with your own money? Improve those scores and get the job!

- **Utility or rental deposits.** During difficult economic times, there tends to be a lot of rental movement. The amount you have to pay down on utilities or the deposit to rent a property is determined by your score.

- **0 percent APR.** Have you ever been tempted by the advertisement on a new car, furniture, or a credit card that offers special 0 percent APR? Do interest rates get any better than that? No wonder so many people line up to sign up for these special deals. But wait a minute! Not so fast! Few people realize that these kinds of special offers only go to those who have the top levels in the national distribution of FICO scores.

- **So close and yet so far.** Sometimes the difference between qualifying for a great deal and not qualifying for it can be as close as twenty points on your FICO score. You may say, "So what? I don't qualify for it. I can still qualify for a fairly low interest rate." Well, it really does add up and it matters a great deal. The difference on a $20,000 car loan at a 0 percent APR versus the standard 7 to 8 percent APR is around $1,800 more over the course of the loan. This is very significant indeed!

- **Insurance rates.** Does having a bad credit rating affect anything other than loans and interest rates? Yes. It could affect what kind of insurance premium you'll pay. Some auto insurers are using credit data to help determine your insurance rates. Ninety-two of the hundred largest personal auto insurance companies in the country use credit data in underwriting new business, according to a study by Conning and Co., an insurance research and asset management firm.

    There does seem to be a connection between your credit score and the likelihood of your having to file an auto insurance claim. It's purely in the numbers. According to a study by the Insurance Information Institute, drivers at the bottom of the credit chart file 40 percent more claims than drivers at the top. A consumer with bad credit is going to pay 20 to 50 percent more in auto insurance premiums than a person who has good credit.

    If you're already insured, then you might want to stay where you are, especially if your credit isn't as great as it could be. Insurance underwriters follow the credit data when reviewing new customers, and far fewer (only 14 percent) national insurers use credit data for renewals. In fact, some states don't allow this practice at all.

So FICO is a credit number, but what is a FICO really?

The score is called FICO because most credit bureau scores use formulas developed by the Fair Isaac Corporation. These scores are provided by the three major credit reporting agencies: Equifax, Experian (formerly TRW), and TransUnion. Because they process the data differently, there may be a slight difference in scores from each reporting agency, but they are usually within a few points of one another.

FICO scores provide the best guide to the kind of credit risk you will be to lenders. Lenders figure that if you have a higher score, you're going to be less risk. This doesn't mean you'll be perceived as a good or bad customer; it's just what the statistics are saying about your financial habits, including available credit, payment history, and credit-to-debt ratios.

There's no magic number that will guarantee you will get a better interest rate or automatically become a low-risk borrower. These numbers are somewhat subjective, as they vary from lender to lender. One lender may feel you need to have a 700 or above to qualify for their card, whereas another lender's cutoff point may be around 550. That's why when you're shopping for loans, you need to get quotes from a variety of lenders.

What different FICO scores look like in terms of a mortgage loan. Following is a chart comparing FICO scores and interest rates on a $150,000, 30-year fixed-rate mortgage:

You can see from this chart that having a good score can not only make the difference between buying the kind of home you want, but also whether you qualify for a mortgage at all and can begin to build wealth through home ownership.

How does your FICO score stack up to the national average?

National distribution of FICO scores

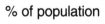
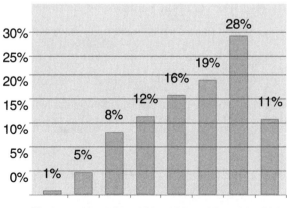

As you can see, 28 percent of Americans have a very good score of 750–799, with 11 percent at the highest range of 800+, while the lowest ranges include the 500–549 range with 5 percent, and the 550–599 with 8 percent.

A low score might mean you'll be denied credit.
The only absolute for credit is that there are no absolutes! While a high FICO makes it reasonable to assume you'll get a particular loan, it doesn't guarantee it any more than a low score guarantees you won't get the loan. A number of factors are involved, including your ability to repay the debt, your credit history, and your employment status and history.

The greatest hits on FICOs, or the items that most negatively impact your credit score, include:

- Late payments
- Bankruptcies
- Collections

Is the current method of credit scoring unfair to minorities?
Yes and no. As mentioned earlier, a woman who does not establish good credit lines on her own and has only co-credit with her spouse may be negatively impacted upon widowhood or divorce. Women who are not the primary providers in the home may have the same problems due to inattention to individual personal credit lines. But as a whole, the credit scoring process is impartial, and the ECOA (Equal Credit Opportunity Act) prohibits lenders from discriminating or considering consumers based on their race, gender, nationality, or marital status.

Will your score take a dip if you apply for new credit?
Applying for new credit should only affect you in a negative way if you open multiple accounts, securing multiple loans simultaneously. For example, let's say you get your dream job with a substantial pay raise and relo-

cate to a much lower cost-of-living area. You could easily buy a new home, new car, and new wardrobe. You decide to get some new clothes right away because that seems like the easiest way to celebrate. The salesperson tells you that you can get a 15 percent discount on that new suit if you open a store charge account, and you think, *I can cancel this after I get it, but that 15 percent is really going to add up on all these clothes for my new job.* You repeat this same pattern at several stores, and you're jazzed about saving so much money with this clever store credit card trick.

Then you go to the car dealership with your friend who is good at negotiating and get a great price on a new car and a super-duper interest rate on the loan. Finally, it's time to go buy your dream home, and since you were told you had a good FICO when you started looking several months ago, you've figured out how much house you can afford at the interest rate you should be able to qualify for. The only problem is that your FICO used to be great, but it's taken a significant hit due to all the credit cards you've opened, the new car you just bought, and the credit inquiries into your account for your new insurance policy. Suddenly, your very manageable mortgage payment, which you estimated to be $851 per month, is now going to be a whopping $1,028 per month due to the fact that you now have a lower FICO score.

So which loans should I secure first if I'm going to get multiple loans?

While one new account may only moderately affect your FICO, multiple accounts for greater debt will hit it hard. Consequently, here is the order you should apply for these loans in order to maximize your credit rating to get the best interest rates on the largest loans:

- Your mortgage loan
- Your car
- Other accounts (including credit cards and the establishing of utilities such as electricity, gas, and water)

*Are you saying that a lower FICO score could cost me
more on my utilities?*

When we bought a new home in California and had not yet sold the
home in New Mexico, we ran into the problem of a dropping FICO
score. We had excellent FICO scores, enough to carry two different sets
of mortgages on two homes, and we were able to get the best mortgage
rate possible. But unbeknownst to me, my husband had taken out a 0
percent APR loan for a hot tub cover and some expensive furniture. We
had agreed on setting the money aside to make these purchases, and we
had the ability to pay the debt immediately. But when Bob walked into
the store, his thought process was *Why not use someone else's money for a
year rather than our own? We can keep our money in investments and come
out ahead.*

He wasn't aware of how multiple accounts hit a FICO. By the time we
secured first and second mortgages plus lines of credit for the consumer
goods, we were told that we had to pay a deposit on our electricity setup
because Bob's credit rating was not as high as it needed to be in order to
waive the deposit!

Consequently, we had to set up the services in my name, under my
FICO score, because I had guarded my credit rating and didn't have the
additional lines of credit open. It can happen to any of us if we're not aware
of the factors involved in FICO scoring.

*You keep talking about the "factors" involved in credit scoring.
What are these?*

There are five basic categories that influence your score:

- **Time.** This is the length of your credit history and the amount
  of time since your accounts were opened. These are viewed and
  ranked by specific types of accounts.

- **New credit.** This is the number of recently opened accounts as well as the number of inquiries into your credit history. This would also include the reestablishment of credit after a bad credit history.
- **Type.** There are five basic kinds of credit accounts: credit cards, mortgage loans, store (or retail) cards, consumer finance accounts, and installment loans (including car loans).
- **Debt load.** This is the number of accounts you have and the proportion of revolving debt to the total amount of credit lines available. These are called debt ratios, and we will discuss these in detail in the next section.
- **History.** This primarily means your payment history, including whether you pay on time, how much you pay down on revolving debt (or whether you pay only the minimums), your payment patterns, whether you've defaulted on loans, and any other bankruptcies or delinquencies. The last three types of entries will be removed from your credit history after a certain period (usually five to seven years).

Here is what it looks like:

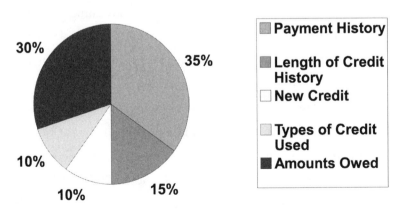

Source: www.myfico.com/myfico/CreditCentral/ScoreConsiders.asp

So how can I have my piece of the pie?

If you have a good FICO score, there's a way to keep it good. And there is also good news if you currently have a bad FICO score—there's room for improvement, and it may happen more quickly than you would think. Here are the basic steps to an improved FICO score:

- **Pay on time.** As you read in chapter 5, some credit cards may have a billing cycle of as little as twenty-one days, so pay your minimum as soon as you get your bill (and send more later), or set it up with your bank to automatically pay the credit card company every month.

- **Check your credit.** Each month when your credit card bill comes, the first thing you need to do is check it for discrepancies. Not only is this an early indicator of possible identity theft, but it also allows you to make sure you're not being tapped with erroneous charges. If you find a discrepancy, then it's important to contact the lender or a credit bureau as soon as possible.

- **Debt ratios.** Part of your scoring depends upon what your debt ratio is—or the amount of debt versus the total amount of credit available to you. According to Bankrate.com, "Credit-scoring models look at a number of factors when calculating your score, including the result of the following formula: the total amount of debt on credit cards and revolving accounts divided by the total amount of debt available on those accounts. The formula results in a fraction less than one. The lower the fraction, the better. A score of one would mean your outstanding debt equals your available credit and you've maxed out your credit cards." An example would be an available credit line of $10,000 and $5,000 in debt. When you divide the total credit by the debt, you have a ratio of half. You're using half of the credit available to you. But if you're using a card with a credit line of $15,000 and you still carry the $5,000 in debt, then you have a better ratio of one-to-three, or one-third of the credit available to you.

- **What you buy.** If you are planning to buy an automobile or a home, the best advice regarding your debt ratio would be to pay down as much debt as possible and don't cancel these lines of credit until after you've secured your larger loan.

- **Time** can be a good thing when it comes to your FICO score. Not only can you improve it over time, but the longer you've had a card, the higher your credit limit is (which helps the ratios we discussed in a previous point), and it also proves a solid credit history. So if you need to cancel a credit card, hang on to those you've had the longest and those that have the highest credit limit. When you have a history of paying your bills on time, paying down revolving balances, and not biting off more debt than you can chew, then you will see a steady increase in your FICO number.

- **Limit inquiries.** Most consumers are not aware of the fact that each time a potential lender inquires into your credit history, you take a hit on your FICO score. This is because a large number of inquiries over a short period of time may indicate that you are opening too many credit accounts due to financial difficulties such as unemployment or an unexpected financial setback. It could also indicate that you are taking on more debt than you can comfortably pay back.

There's a really good chance that you've just gained new knowledge about how FICO scores work and how they can be used as an effective tool in helping your family get what they need without going into greater debt and becoming a "servant to the lender." Why not go a step further and allow the takeaway portion of this chapter be something you can act on this week? Write down your goals for improving your FICO, and take one step a week for the next six weeks—tracking your FICO as you go to see the improvement. You may be pleasantly surprised at the positive results and feel more empowered to be in control of your debt weight than ever before. Just do me a favor. Don't go out and charge a new suit to celebrate. Pay cash instead.

I've shared a lot of information in this chapter, and I'm hoping you'll see two things:

1. FICOs are very important.
2. I can help or hurt my score.

Your score may be a lot easier to improve that you think. Of all the factors mentioned in this section, three stand out as particularly easy to do and effective when you do them. If you do the following things and *don't* do any of the other things that will hurt your credit (like crank up new debt or apply for another loan), then I promise you you'll see an improvement in a couple of months.

Living Rich Questions

What is your FICO score? Go to myFICO.com to find out!
What aspects of your life does your FICO score impact?
How does your FICO score stack up to the national average?

7

The 10/10/80 Budget for "Special" People

How to Develop a Workable Plan

If we command our wealth, we shall be rich and free.
If our wealth commands us, we are poor indeed.
EDMUND BURKE

Yesterday my husband was looking for the milk. He just bought a gallon at the store and knew we had some.

He found it inside the kitchen pantry, on the shelf—at room temp.

Then he tried to find the checkbook.

It was on a back patio chair—dripping wet from when the sprinklers went on.

He tried to brush his teeth.

But his toothbrush was covered with shoe polish.

He went to his dresser to get his new undies.

But they were pink (having been accidentally washed with a red beret).

He got in the car to go to work (after I borrowed his car that weekend).

The gas was below empty, and on flashed the oil and service lights.

He got to work and opened his e-mail.

He found notification that the check used to pay the kids' tuition was not signed.

He went to eat a quick lunch before his continuation flight (he's a test pilot), and in his lunch bag he found two apples, a bottle of water, and a Quaker granola bar. (His son got two sandwiches, a bottle of water, and a Quaker granola bar.)

I won't bore you with the rest of his day, and my guy will never tell you this—he's too smart to actually say it. But…

…my husband has a "special" wife—a woman on a deadline.

Part of my distracted behavior happens when I'm overtasked with too many things to do and too few hours in my day. I'm not alone in these feelings of being overwhelmed at times. I know you've felt the pressure of all the things you need to do and what is expected of you. We all experience these feelings of an impending trip to the funny farm. How do we do it all? We're supposed to give things away, we're supposed to save money, and we're supposed to live on a budget as well. Can we really live like this?

That's why I developed a financial plan for busy people. This is good news for "special" people like me—the 10/10/80 Budget is designed for you, the overwhelmed and distracted. It is simple to set up, easy to use, and adjustable to meet your family's unique needs. It has worked for us for the last twenty years, and it will work for you as well. By following this plan, you can learn to Live Rich for Less.

The 10/10/80 Budget

We've talked about the 10/10/80 Rule for your finances, and budgeting is the primary area where this rule comes alive. It is structured as follows:

- 10 percent: Give generously.
- 10 percent: Save diligently.
- 80 percent: Spend wisely.

Friendly Reminders to Special People

Some things to keep in mind as you develop your financial plan (in the chart of the 10/10/80 Budget):

1. **Set goals.** Begin with the end in mind. If you don't know where your family finances are going, how can you reach your desired destination? Goals are a road map to where you want to be.

2. **Be honest.** When you calculate current spending levels to determine your current budget, be sure to write down everything you spend, including cash, over a three-month period. This will help you discover how you are currently spending your money. You'll be able to recognize the excess right away and see where your problem areas are.

3. **Calculate your 10/10/80 Budget.** Now that you've seen where all the money is going, it's time to redirect that money into some giving, saving, and spending that will help your family Live Rich for Less.

4. **Measure your progress regularly.** Continue to keep records, and once a quarter, assess your progress toward your financial goals. Are you paying down debt? Are you giving to your community? Are you building your savings accounts? During these evaluation sessions, you may need to reassess either your goals or your plan.

5. **No worries, mon!** When I went to Jamaica on a writers' cruise, I chose the shore excursion called zip-lining. We strapped on a harness, attached a metal loop to our belts, and rode lines attached to 100-foot tree canopies in the jungle. The Jamaican guides would smile reassuringly and say, "No worries, mon! It will be all right!" Having a confident, relaxed view of your plan will help you achieve your goals.

The most important aspect of the 10/10/80 Budget is that you tailor it for your family. For example, you might drive a company car, so your automobile expenses are slightly lower than average. You could take this overage and carry it over to the servicing of consumer debt. Or you may need to take measures to cut your food budget or shop around on insurance to arrive at a workable budget for your family.

Your expenses may vary according to your geographic location. People living in the north may have higher utility bills due to their harsh winters. People in the south may have greater electricity bills due to air conditioning in the summer. Our family has higher education costs because of the number of children. It's important to realize that although there is some uniformity in the basic 10/10/80 Budget, you will also need to make it uniquely yours.

The Big Give: 10 Percent

If you want to live rich, here is your first big test. You will need to commit the first 10 percent of your budget to a nonprofit of your choice. We've thoroughly discussed the whys and hows of this in earlier chapters, and now is the time to put it to paper and decide to give away your first 10 percent. It worked for Warren Buffet and Bill Gates; it will work for you as well.

The Big Save: 10 Percent

This is where you pay yourself, and it's a critical part of accumulating wealth to live the rich life. Allocate this from your paycheck before you even see it—a portion may go directly to your savings account and/or to fund your 401(k). If you never see this money in your take-home pay, it's a lot easier to let it grow in your savings vehicle and adjust your spending levels to live within your means.

The Big Spend: 80 Percent

It's hard to say which category is the most challenging in the 10/10/80 Budget. For some, it may be giving away that first 10 percent—they're just not used to that kind of generosity. For others it may be saving the next 10 percent, as there generally seems to be some bill that needs to be paid out of the savings account. But it has been my experience that this final part of the budget, the big spend, can solve the other category problems if you simply learn to spend smarter and live within your means. A few steps are involved in putting together the 10/10/80 Budget. Let's look at them individually.

Step 1: Calculate Your Income

The first step is to determine household income *after* state and federal income taxes and Social Security. Income includes salary, rents, notes, interest, dividends, tips, child support, and other forms of income. Enter the total on the line Net Income on the budget form included in this section.

Step 2: Calculate *Current* Spending Levels

The next step is to calculate your *current* spending patterns. Perhaps you don't have a budget at all, or you aren't giving or saving. You may even find yourself in more debt each month through credit card spending. Fill in your current spending levels in the chart, and be prepared for a reality check!

If you prefer online tools, then after you've worked through the 10/10/80 Budget chart at the end of this chapter and decided on a workable giving/saving/spending plan, you can go to Msnmoney.com, Motleyfool.com, or Crown.org to find a tool that will help meet your techie needs.

The 10/10/80 Budget

Account Name	Current Budget	Difference Between Current and New	New 10/10/80 Budget
Giving/Tithes/ Contributions 10 percent			
Savings 10 percent			
Spending Totals 80 percent			
Food 10 percent			
Clothing/ Dry Cleaning 5 percent			
Education/ Miscellaneous 5 percent			
Housing/Utilities/ Taxes 30 percent			
Insurance 5 percent			
Medical/Dental 4 percent			
Recreation/ Vacation/Gifts 6 percent			
Transportation 15 percent			
Net Income			

Step 3: Calculate Your Current Situation

Now take your net income and subtract your current spending to establish your overall family spending. Are you spending more (through credit) than you net each month? Are you spending everything you make (with nothing going into savings)? Are there unexplained gaps in your current spending levels? Did you know you were hitting the ATM machine that many times each month or getting that much cash back on your debit card purchases? Are you saving as much as you need to? Or, are you on target and healthy in your current giving, saving, and spending patterns?

Step 4: Determine Your 10/10/80 Budget Based
on Line Items

As you prepare to fill in your budget form, it's important to know what kinds of expenses are included in each category and to list any items your family has that are unique to your situation. Here is a basic detailed list of line items that should be included in each category.

- Tithe/Charitable Donations: 10 percent to church, civic, or community donations
- Savings: 10 percent to savings accounts, 401(k) funding, Roth IRA, or other IRA investments, regular savings for upcoming bills (insurance, taxes, etc.), and emergencies
- Clothing/Dry Cleaning: 5 percent to new clothing and shoes, thrift store bargains, garage sale finds, dry cleaning, alterations, repairs, patterns, and sewing supplies
- Education/Miscellaneous: 5 percent to tuition, books, music or other lessons, school supplies, newspapers, and miscellaneous expenses. The miscellaneous portion includes all other unbudgeted items and any debt payments
- Food: 10 percent to groceries and meals eaten outside the home

- Housing: 30 percent to mortgage or rent, property taxes, utilities (including phone, gas, water, and electricity), cleaning supplies, labor costs/maid, lawn care, pool care, tools and repair, household repairs, furniture and bedding, appliances, and garden equipment
- Insurance: 5 percent assumes some employee health insurance benefits. It also includes life, house, and health insurance copays and deductibles
- Medical/Dental: 4 percent to doctor, dentist, eyeglasses, medicines, and vitamins
- Recreation/Vacation/Gifts: 6 percent to entertainment, movies, hobbies, pets, television, sporting goods, toys, gifts, and vacations
- Transportation: 15 percent to airline fares, bus and taxi fares, car payments and insurance, car repairs and licenses, gasoline, and oil

Budgeting is kind of an adventure. There are boundaries, rules, and guidelines that work if you follow them carefully. But don't get discouraged if your current spending patterns are not where they will one day be as you continue toward your goal to follow the 10/10/80 Budget.

The next few chapters will show you how to painlessly reduce spending levels in all major categories, setting you up for success! It really is possible, with the right attitude and desire, to live rich for less.

Living Rich Questions

Do you currently have a budget, and do you live by it?

Does your current budget allow for giving and saving?

When you calculate your current giving/saving/spending patterns, how far do you have to go to reach the 10/10/80 Budget goal? Are you willing to take the initial steps to begin to achieve this budget goal?

Part 3

Spending Smart the Other 80 Percent

The smartest dollar you ever make is the one you spend well

Before I was a SAHM (stay-at-home mom) I was a SWF (single white female) businesswoman (BW). As you may already know, I was a SWF BW from the time I was seven years old and had my first home-based business. At that time of pigtails and buckteeth, I never even thought of being a SAHM. So when I married an AF (air force) fighter pilot and he introduced me to a world of acronyms, like TDY (temporary duty) and PCS (permanent change of station), I was right at home. Well, kind of.

Even though I loved the SAHM gig and really loved my family, I still missed being a BW. In fact, I had an identity crisis of sorts when there were no longer deals to close, customers to market, and portfolios to expand. For a while I lived vicariously through my SAWH (stay-at-work husband) and learned all the nuances of the politics of the royal military court. I went to countless social events, formal parties, and military ceremonies. I heard way too many fighter pilots say things like, "Enough talk about flying, let's talk about *me*."

Yawn.

I needed something more. Finally, I decided I could become a SAHM BW and made my new work the "business" of saving money. I treated my job as a profession, much to the amusement of Bob's pilot peers. They would smile indulgently as if they wanted to pat me on the head and say, "There, there. Sure, your profession is saving money. Now run along, honey, and get me some of those cheese puff thingies you made for the party."

But I had the last laugh indeed: If you treat a job like a profession, it will eventually become one.

But this didn't happen overnight. I had to start small. I started as a jack-of-all-trades and master of one: couponing. But as a superhero is prone to do, the coupon gig was only a cover—underneath I was "America's Family Financial Expert" waiting to emerge to guide Mr. and Ms. America to their present mission. I believe that you have the ability within you to bring your spending habits to a professional level—one that will dictate what you do with the bulk of your money, honey. It's the 80 percent that requires all the smarts of a BW, the ingenuity of a savvy SAHM, and the perseverance of a fighter pilot. But you can do it.

This final section will discuss how cool it is to have a rich lifestyle and pay less. There are easy, practical, and new ways to save big on everything that touches your world—from insurance to vacations, from cars to corn, from your home to your health. Plus, the final area discusses how to really live it up in the richest way possible—by leaving a legacy through your very own Cha Ching Factor. You'll be singing a new song.

Before Liza Minnelli had one too many husbands, she used to be famous for singing, "It's not where you start, it's where you finish." I used to love that song when I was a SWF BW, but when I got to be a SAHM, I realized it would be a long time before I finished.

In the meantime, I had a lot of living and loving to do as well as lessons that needed to be learned in the process. I'm content with the journey and want to live rich along the way. I don't want to wait until I finish to live well—I want it now and can have it now! But when the finish line is near, I want to do it well—leaving a legacy that still sings.

So, Mr. and Ms. America, let's continue with the finish in mind but purpose to enjoy the spoils of living rich for less along the way.

8

The New Cool

Slashing Insurance Costs, and Room-by-Room Cash Savings

Just think how happy you would be if you lost everything you have right now and then got it back again.

FRANCES RODMAN

I sat on the edge of my desk in seventh period Spanish class listening to *la profesora* just hablah, blah, blah about verb conjugations. The only noise I wanted to hear was the bell that would end my high school day. This class was an easy A, as my Spanish mom had already taught me what she considered the basics of the language—specifically that *por favor* means "please" and that *de nada* means "you're welcome." Then of course her favorite was, *"Mi mamá es hermosa y elegante,"* meaning, "My mom is beautiful and smart." For the longest time I thought that meant my mom had an elegant mustache. By the time I was in high school, I knew there was nothing elegant about Latinas with mustaches.

Little did my mom know that my older cousins had taught me a few more things when I'd stayed with them in Spain the summer before. For example, I knew that *"Él no fumaba y no fijó el bote de basura en el fuego"* means "He *wasn't* smoking and did not set the trash can on fire." I also learned the ever important *"Necesito más dinero"* meant "I need more money, por favor."

No, I wasn't too interested in Spanish class. As soon as that bell rang, it was *"¡Arriba! ¡Arriba!"* racing Speedy Gonzales for the door and shouting *adiós* to Profesora Bora. I also said *hola* to a deep, dark secret passion waiting for me at home while my mom and dad were still at work.

No one knew about this undercover indulgence. I kept it carefully hidden from the other dancers on my drill team, from nosy siblings, and even from my best friend, Donna. In fact, I'm sure that when she reads this chapter, she'll be shocked and say, "Oh my! I never knew."

I had an addiction. I was hooked on… *The Frugal Gourmet.*

To me, the Frugal Gourmet was so manly, marvelous, and miserly. He created an eggplant casserole for pennies per serving and whipped up a chocolate pecan pie for less than $1.50. Yes, he was my dreamboat. I put him on a white horse, far ahead of the—widely popular Galloping Gourmet. No, my guy was clever, creative…and cheap!

Within a few months, I heard just how cheap he was, which rocked my view of this icon forever. I saw a television exposé that painted the Frugal Gourmet as "difficult to work with" and someone who "grossly underpaid his people." My heart sank as a journalist interviewed one of the Gourmet's former staff members, who had launched the lawsuit against him.

"If you want to work for a guy who defines frugal as freakishly cheap and a tightwad who would charge his mom for tickets to his show—then by all means, apply right away to work for the Frugal Gourmet," the former staffer said.

I learned a lot of things that day. Like that hanging out with the boring Profesora Bora was better than discovering that your hero was a heel. That impressionable teenager also learned that people tend to look at the terms *frugal, cheap,* and *miserly* as dirty words.

That was problematic because I was born saving money. It couldn't be hidden—I, too, was freakishly frugal! But I also gave money to orphans in third-world countries and free rides in my car to my girlfriends. There was no need for them to pay for my gas. No, I wasn't cheap. I could live well and still save money. It was then that I realized that by spending smart I could have luxuries that other kids my age didn't have, like a car. So it was possible to live rich, and I didn't have to accept the distinction of being "cheap" in order to accomplish this goal.

Today, I don't use the negative tag lines associated with saving money, such as *cheapskate, frugal,* or *miserly.* It's just not cool to me, baby! In fact, I was interviewed by *USA Today* for a front-page feature about trends indicating that saving money is the new cool. I believe that's true! Sometimes people don't want to learn how to trim costs because it seems cheesy, or they think it means doing weird things like saving bits of foil, reusing your coffee grounds (for more coffee), or harvesting your own fertilizer. Um, I've actually seen people do all of these things in order to "save money." Not I. There are ways to save money that won't embarrass your family or annoy your friends.

It's cool, not cheap, to learn how to do more with less and live well while on a budget. It's a hip way to keep your money from saying adiós before you've had a chance to put it in a savings account. It's also the best way to recession-proof your household, learning quick and easy ways to cut back on regular expenses while surviving and thriving with a comfortable lifestyle. But you have to be proactive. Living rich for less won't just… happen. You'll find, however, that a lot of these steps are much easier to take than you originally thought. So are you ready to save money, be cool, and still find a way to live rich for less?

Reassure When You Insure

What is one thing you need to have but hope you will never use? Insurance. When you want to recession-proof your life, it's important to cover the big areas of spending that can yield the maximum savings for the minimum amount of time—insurance is one of these areas where it's easy to recession-proof your life.

As a former insurance broker, I actively looked for ways to help people cut costs, and doing this almost doubled the number of policies our agency had in force in just a few short years! One of the things I learned along the way was that many insurance choices are "pay me now or pay me later." Some families buy the wrong coverage and end up paying for their own losses, while others pay for more protection than they need. Following are the top ten ways to cut the insurance fat and still maintain the right kind of coverage for your financial body type.

1. Homeowners Save More

Most people have their homeowner's insurance paid as part of the mortgage payment and don't think to get an annual review on this policy. Every year, a family should ask their agent how to reduce costs through discounts for nonsmokers, fire prevention devices in the home, security systems, or a new tile roof. Carry only the coverage needed. Most families should carry the Homeowners Broad Form and only up to 90 percent of the home's value—*don't* include the land in this coverage. You can't collect more than the home value if there is total loss, so don't pay for additional premiums. Further reduce premiums by increasing the deductible to $500, $1,000, or 1 percent of the total amount of coverage.

2. Replacement Insurance for Optimum Value

There should be *replacement value* on personal property insurance. It only costs a little more, and the additional coverage is worthwhile. For example, if the pipes freeze and permanently damage the carpet, replacement value will reimburse the cost of replacing it with the same quality carpet—less

Real Ways to Save on Gas

- Prices. Go to sites such as Gaspricewatch.com, and find the cheapest price for gas both at home and en route.
- Pace your driving. Jackrabbit starts and constant speeding up and slowing down cost precious gas mileage. Instead pace yourself.
- Pushing it up! Speeding will only speed up your fuel consumption. According to the Department of Energy, it takes a lot of energy for your vehicle to push the air out of the way as you speed down the road. Driving 65 versus 75 can save as much as 15 percent on fuel consumption because of the energy needed for higher speeds.
- Puhleeze give me some air. At speeds of 40 miles per hour or greater, it costs more to leave the windows open (due to drag) than it does to run the air. In our California town the summer temps reach 110 degrees, so that's good news!
- Pitch the junk! Take your golf clubs, soccer chairs, Salvation Army book donations, and all the other *junk* out of your *trunk.* Otherwise you're paying more to haul it.
- Pressurize and maintain. Make sure you have the correct air pressure in your tires, and maintain your vehicle with regular tune-ups to save another 5 percent.
- Premium, schmemium. According to AAA, only 5 percent of vehicles in the U.S. require premium gas—it does not help your vehicle to pay more for it. Buy the regular stuff and have no worries.
- Change your air filters regularly.

the deductible. If there's no replacement value, the carpet will be depreciated, which won't leave much of a check to cover the damages.

3. Pretty and Precious

When you evaluate your policy, it's wise to consider a Personal Articles Rider/Floater for replacement value on those precious items. If a thief steals jewelry, guns, computer equipment, antiques, coin collections, and other personal items, the homeowner's insurance could cover as little as $500 unless these things are *itemized.* The cost of this additional coverage depends upon the total amount of the rider. When the average value of a woman's jewelry in America is estimated at $5,600, this tip could save you over $5,000 if a thief decides to pay your house a visit while you're at the movies.

4. Identity Theft Protection

Identity theft can happen anywhere to anyone—in line at the store, online, at home, or when you're buying your morning coffee. If your identity is stolen, you can spend hundreds of hours cleaning up your credit and struggling to get back your good name. That's because stolen identities are often used up to thirty times, with most victims discovering the theft only after they've been turned down for a loan or contacted by a collection agency. You may already be a victim many times over and not even know it. Some homeowners' policies offer identity theft protection that usually costs about $50 per year, but they may not offer the measure of tracking that can stop this negative action before it begins.

5. Beep! Beep! Car Insurance Cheap!

Your mama said you should drive the speed limit, and insurance companies agree. Each ticket and each accident add surcharge points and additional premiums to the cost of a policy. So if you were given a ticket unfairly, it pays to fight it. If another person was at fault in an accident, call the police to the scene to write a police report that proves no fault and removes any surcharge points on the policy. Go for higher deductibles on comprehensive and collision in order to insure big accidents, not fender benders.

6. Compare and Beware

Secure estimates from at least three major companies before purchasing automobile insurance. Reduce the cost of insurance on your car by buying the right kind of car. Some vehicles are far more expensive to insure than others, so check with an insurance agent before buying. If possible, use the least expensive car to travel to and from work. "For pleasure only" is the rating used for SAHMs (stay-at-home moms), and it is one of the least expensive ratings, so use that on the most expensive vehicle.

7. Get All That's Coming to You—Discounts!

Some companies offer discounts to nonsmokers and/or nondrinkers (total abstainers). Other discounts can possibly be included for antitheft devices, safe drivers, multicar discounts, drivers between ages thirty and sixty, or driver's education courses. Certain professions, such as the military, are sometimes given special discounts. Other companies offer a discount if you carry your homeowner's insurance with them.

8. Youthful-Driver Dilemmas

Carefully consider when a teenager gets his or her driver's license. Once teens have a license, even if they don't have a car to drive, they'll have to be listed somewhere on the policy. If the only cars on the policy are fully covered vehicles (comprehensive and collision), it could double the premiums!

The best option is to put a teenager as the principal driver on an older vehicle that only carries the basic package—liability, medical, and uninsured motorists. Consider letting the teen pay a portion (or all) of his insurance premium—it's an extra incentive to drive safely.

9. Protection, Not Investment

Life insurance is a supplementary provision for the family—not an investment. That is why it's better to consider buying term rather than whole life insurance. The chart provided on page 167 has a complete analysis, but it is generally more affordable to buy term and invest the difference, rather than pay the higher prices of permanent (or whole) life insurance. There should be enough insurance to pay off debts with adequate principal for the family to live modestly off the interest. For competitive insurance quotes, call Select Quote at (800) 343-1985, or go to Insure.com.

10. Health Insurance

The best and least expensive medical insurance could be from your employer, especially if they pay your premium. This is usually a group policy offering special rates that include dependents, but the rate for your dependents is worth shopping. A good health insurance plan should cover 80 percent of the medical bills in the event of a major illness. If you lose your job, you *might* be able to maintain your insurance (go to Cobra health.com for details).

An excellent online source for insurance comparisons is Ehealth insurance.com. This site researches the optimum plan for your needs and provides the best price because they offer carrier-direct rates with real-time quotes. They also research health insurance providers and policy rates for dental and life insurance.

Go to the library and look at the magazine *Best's Insurance Reports* to

Everything You Wanted to Know About Life Insurance

Type of Insurance	*Advantages	+Disadvantages
Level Term	*Level payments over specific period, usually 5, 10, 15, or 20 years; may be convertible to a permanent policy.	+More expensive than ART (see below) in early years; less expensive in later years.
Whole Life (permanent)	*Fixed premiums; cash value you can borrow against; possible dividends; tax-deferred earnings; guaranteed death benefits.	+Initially higher premium than term insurance; little flexibility in premium payments.
Universal Life (permanent)	*Flexible premiums; tax-deferred earning on cash value; accessible funds; different options allow cash buildup or insurance protection.	+If interest rates fall, low cash-value buildup may cause policy to lapse unless you add money.
Variable Life (permanent)	*Fixed, level premiums; guaranteed death benefit; choice of investment options.	+Premiums start low but rise with each new term; nothing back if you outlive contract.
Annual Renewable Term (ART)	*Most coverage for the least money; protection in increments of one year; can renew yearly up to specified age (usually 70); may be convertible to permanent policy.	+Potentially higher earnings than other cash-value policies but also greater risk.
Variable Universal Life (permanent)	*Similar to variable life but with flexible payments.	+You select the investment vehicle that generates your cash value growth (stocks, bonds, etc.), so there's greater risk.

find the latest information on A-rated companies. Some self-employed people use Golden Rule, now a part of United Healthcare (Goldenrule .com), as an option. Consider raising major medical deductibles to $1,000, and make sure the plan has a no-deductible accident provision. Never buy two policies on one person—you pay twice, but you can't collect twice! Don't cancel an existing policy until a new one is in place, or there may be a gap in coverage. Make sure to check out Ehealthinsurance.com for a quote from a provider in your area.

Health Savings Accounts

Health Savings Accounts could possibly be a great option for you. Congress passed legislation that makes paying for medical expenses much more affordable for consumers. The law provides broad access to Health Savings Accounts, or HSAs, which allow consumers to pay for qualified medical expenses with pretax dollars (income tax–free!) and save for retirement on a tax-deferred basis.

Basically, an HSA is a tax-favored savings account that is used in conjunction with a high-deductible HSA-eligible health insurance plan to make health care more affordable and to save for retirement.

- Pretax money is deposited each year into an HSA and can be easily withdrawn at any time with no penalty or taxes to pay for qualified medical expenses. Withdrawals can also be made for nonmedical purposes but will be taxed as normal income and are subject to a 10 percent penalty if done prior to age sixty-five.
- Any HSA funds not used each year remain in the account and earn interest tax-free to supplement medical expenses at any time in the future.

- Like an IRA, the account belongs to you, not your employer.
  But unlike an IRA, your employer *can* contribute to your
  HSA.

HSAs can be used to pay for many types of medical expenses, even some that are often excluded on health insurance plans. These include:

- Health insurance plan deductibles, copayments, and coinsurance
- Prescription and over-the-counter drugs
- Dental services, including braces, bridges, and crowns
- Vision care, including glasses and LASIK eye surgery
- Psychiatric and certain psychological treatments
- Long-term care services
- Medically related transportation and lodging

Typically, HSAs cannot be used to pay health insurance premiums, although there are exceptions for the following:

- Health insurance premiums if you are receiving federal or state unemployment benefits
- Premiums for COBRA-qualified health insurance
- Long-term-care insurance premiums
- Premiums for a health plan (other than a Medicare supplemental policy for an individual age sixty-five or older)

One important footnote is that you must establish an HSA before incurring any expenses, or the expenses will not qualify.

But not all health insurance plans qualify to be used in conjunction with HSAs, only those that are eligible. This type of insurance plan is often referred to as a High Deductible Health Plan (HDHP) and is typically less expensive than plans with lower deductibles. The following criteria must be met to be considered HSA-eligible:

- The plan must have an annual deductible of at least $1,000 for individuals and at least $2,000 for families.

- The sum of the annual deductible and the other annual out-of-pocket expenses required to be paid under the plan (other than premiums) should not exceed $5,000 for individuals and $10,000 for families.

For a complete list of HSA-eligible plans or to investigate signing up for one of these savings accounts, go to Ehealthinsurance.com. Since the funds you put into this account are carried over each year, the worst-case scenario is that you remain quite healthy and use the HSA very little. In that case you'd have more money in that account growing tax-free until you're sixty-five years old, and then you could withdraw it without paying taxes. Sounds like a win-win deal to me!

Room-by-Room Savings

One of the reasons the average American family is not recession-proof is because they live a consumptive lifestyle, and this is particularly true at home. Here are some ways to experience the thrill of saving money room by room:

Kitchen

- **Combine oven dishes.** Select menu items that will cook at the same temperature rather than heating the oven twice at two different temps. This can save $125 in energy costs.
- **Cloth napkins and real plates.** Although it's less convenient, it's cheaper to wash than to buy paper. This tip saves almost $95 per year.
- **Quality paper products.** Sometimes the cheaper versions of paper products end up costing you far more. The Bounty paper towels I use are 25 percent thicker and clothlike, making it easier to handle my cleaning needs. I use fewer sheets because I just rinse, wring,

and reopen to get tougher jobs done—this saves me money in the long run. By using half as many towels as the leading store brand, this kind of purchase saves me about $50 a year!

- Check **seals on your refrigerator** and clean the coils to save $50 per year on energy costs.

Family Room

- **Coverings.** If you still have young children at home, you may want to wait to have your furniture re-covered. By purchasing a quality slipcover for $65 instead of buying a new sofa for $850, you save $785. By placing a crocheted doily for $15 on the coffee table to cover scratches made by a speeding Corvette (Hot Wheels–size!), you save $115 over buying a new table for $130.

- **Quick cleaning.** Spills on carpeting and furniture are best attacked as soon as they happen. It's a wise idea to keep carpet and upholstery cleaner nearby, and be sure your babysitter knows how to use it too. If the carpet must be professionally cleaned, it will cost about $95 more than using a $15 can of cleaner.

- **Consolidate.** Magazines that are taking up space could possibly be consolidated or even canceled. Consider sharing a subscription with a friend or relative; the average American subscribes to two to three magazines that they never read. This can save $90 per year.

Baby's Room

Consider making your own baby wipes to save $140 per year per baby. I did this for all five of our children until they were well into their toddler years. Here's the recipe:

1 round plastic container with lid (about 6 inches tall and wide
   enough to accommodate ½ roll of paper towels)
1 roll of Bounty heavy-duty paper towels (no cheap store
   brands)
4 tablespoons baby oil
4 tablespoons baby shampoo
4 tablespoons baby bath
1 to 2 cups of water (depending on the absorbency of the towel)

Cut a small X (about an inch long) in the plastic lid of the container. Cut the paper towels in half to make two short rolls of towels (use one and save one). Put the first three ingredients in the bottom of the container and add one cup of water. Stir well. Place the paper towel, cut side up, in the water for a few minutes. Then turn it over, cut side down, to let the other side absorb the liquid. Let sit for five minutes. If the roll of paper towels still has dry portions on it, then keeping adding water, ½ cup at a time, at five-minute intervals, until towels are completely damp (not dripping, just damp). After the cardboard center of the paper towel tube is wet, gently pull it out of the center of the towels. Pull the towels from the center, and thread through the X in the lid of the plastic container. Seal. Will keep fresh for up to one month.

Bathrooms

- **Saving water.** Don't put bricks in your toilet tanks to displace water—they could decompose and clog up your pipes. Instead use a one-quart plastic container that will not interfere with the flapper valve and will save as much as $150 per year.
- **Linens.** Buy the same color towels and linens to save big bucks every year. If you choose white towels, then you won't have to

buy a new set if one is stained or mildewed. The same goes for sheets—choose all white and you'll only have to buy a top sheet or a fitted sheet if one is torn or damaged. This can save $55 a year on towels and $85 a year on sheets.

- **Repair now, save later.** Broken tiles and chipped grout in the bathroom should be fixed immediately in order to minimize water damage to tiles and the wallboard. The average replacement after major damage costs $350 compared to a $30 repair, for a savings of $320.

Garage

When it comes to gas mileage and urban legends, you've gotten the e-mails that tell you all kinds of things: To save money at the pump you need to pump the gas slowly, buy gas in the morning, only buy the top half of the tank, or never gas up when there's a truck delivering fuel.

The other part of the e-mail is a boycott of sorts that tells you we can get the price of fuel down by not buying from companies that get oil from the Middle East. If you don't take their advice, then you're either a fuel hog (by not saving money on gas) or you're anti-American (by not boycotting the Middle East.)

The list goes on and on. I checked out this one at my favorite urban legend site, Snopes.com, and guess what? The list is a bunch of horse-feathers!

Buying at certain stations will not only cost you more money, but it also won't reduce the price of Middle Eastern oil—*nada,* zilch. Following all the rituals for buying your gas cannot be proven either. There are much easier (and more painless) options for pruning back prices at the pump. See the Cha Ching Factor on page 163 for the lowdown.

Living Rich Questions

Will you take fifteen minutes this week to make one phone call
to your insurance agent to possibly save hundreds of dollars
this year?

Will you make a phone call to your insurance company and ask
for discounts for your auto and homeowner's policies?

Will you pick one room from our list and save money on one
item from that list? Remember that every little bit helps!

9

Shopping to Save

Shop-Till-You-Drop Savings on Groceries, on Clothing, and Online

By desiring little, a poor man makes himself rich.

DEMOCRITUS

As we made our way toward the grocery store checkout, my eleven-year-old son, Jonathan, said, "Can I go through the line with my stuff by myself?"

I looked at our freckle-faced boy, his eyes lit up with excitement. He was buying groceries for his sister and her new husband as the newlyweds set up the pantry in their first home.

"Sure, son. I'll be here when you're done."

After a few minutes, I heard a commotion in Jonathan's lane—the store manager, the checker, and the bagger were excited.

When Jonathan finished, he was holding three grocery bags, and I asked him, "Honey, what happened over there?"

He smiled broadly. "Well, my total before coupons was $28.60, but afterwards it was only $1.80! They had a hard time believing I could save that much!"

If an eleven-year-old can learn to save that much green in the grocery store, then so can you.

There truly is an art to shopping, one that will save you hundreds at the grocery store, the discount department store, and the mall. This entire section was how I started to make saving money a profession, my job while I stayed home with kids. I know that pinching pennies on groceries can seem mundane and even a bit pedantic, but it can truly add up to a heck of a lot of money—our family saves over $8,000 a year on food, toiletries, and cleansers. Let's see, that's a savings of $8,000 each year for twenty years, or a $160,000 savings.

That puts saving money while shopping in a new light, huh? The ideas in this chapter will help you shop smarter in the grocery store and in the mall, learn to negotiate like an apprentice, and make the most of girl time when shopping with a friend.

Food Funds, Saving Money on Groceries

Store Cards
These are sometimes referred to as "clipless coupons." Sign up for the card at the customer service desk, and as it is scanned at the checkout, you'll receive all the store's special values for the week.

Sale Ads
The store's weekly sale ads either come in the mail or are part of the midweek newspaper inserts. Match up the sale ads with some of the other savings factors listed, and you'll soon find yourself with products for pennies.

Manufacturers' Coupons
These are traditional coupons issued and reimbursed by the manufacturer. If you read the fine print on the coupon, you'll see the manufacturer's name and mailing address. Here are a few places to find these coupons:

- **FSIs, or Free-Standing Inserts.** Most of these are found in the Sunday paper.
- **Blinkers** are the blinking dispensers in the grocery store aisles that dispense coupons for your convenience.
- **Products** that have coupons right on them to be torn off and used immediately. Others require that you purchase the item to retrieve the coupons inside the box or cut them from the packaging.
- **Electronic** coupons are issued at the checkout after you've purchased your groceries. They are usually competitor coupons that are automatically issued as a result of your choices.

Double Coupons

Some stores offer double coupons. This is where the coupon is worth twice the face value—a 50-cent coupon is now worth $1.00. Each store issues limitations, such as "only double up to $1.00," so check the customer service desk for details. Go to the Links page at Elliekay.com to find a link listing all the stores that double coupons in your state.

Unadvertised Sales and Clearances

Check the store aisles for sales and clearance tags. As much as 50 percent of the week's sales are not advertised.

Price Guarantees

Why shop all over town looking for loss leaders when you don't have to? A loss leader is the lead-off sale price for items on the front page of the store circular. When you take all these "best price" sales to a store like Super Wal-Mart, you will be guaranteed the lowest price and get the equivalent of all those sales in one place. Just remember that they do not honor competitors' ads for percent discounts; buy one, get one free; or cash back. Just straight-out matches for the lowest price—guaranteed. This saves you time, gas, money, and stress!

Web Bucks

When items with coupons good for "cash off your next shopping trip" are purchased, you will automatically get these invaluable cash-off coupons.

Official USDA Food Plans: Cost of Food at Home at Four Levels, U.S. Average, June 2007

Age-gender groups	Weekly cost			Monthly cost		
	Low-cost plan	Moderate-cost plan	Liberal plan	Low-cost plan	Moderate-cost plan	Liberal plan
Individuals						
Child:						
1 year	24.40	28.10	34.00	105.80	121.90	147.50
2 years	23.90	28.40	34.30	103.60	123.00	148.80
3-5 years	26.20	32.20	39.10	113.40	139.50	169.50
6-8 years	35.50	43.80	51.40	154.00	190.00	222.70
9-11 years	39.90	50.90	59.60	173.10	220.60	258.10
Male:						
12-14 years	45.10	55.70	66.10	195.60	241.50	286.30
15-19 years	46.70	57.80	67.40	202.30	250.50	292.10
20-50 years	46.20	57.40	70.30	200.20	248.70	304.60
51 years and over	43.80	54.00	65.10	189.80	234.20	282.10
Female:						
12-19 years	39.10	47.10	57.30	169.20	204.20	248.10
20-50 years	40.20	49.10	63.30	174.10	212.70	274.10
51 years and over	39.00	48.50	58.30	168.90	210.20	252.50
Families						
Family of 2:						
20-50 years	95.00	117.10	146.90	411.60	507.50	636.50
51 years and over	91.10	112.80	135.70	394.60	488.80	588.00
Family of 4:						
Couple, 20-50 years and children						
2 and 3-5 years	136.50	167.00	207.00	591.30	723.80	896.90
6-8 and 9-11 years	161.80	201.20	244.50	701.30	871.80	1059.50

Source: www.cnpp.usda.gov

When I shopped on the show *Good Morning, Texas,* the total before coupons was $127. After coupons, I paid $22 and received $20 in Web bucks that could be used on my next trip—now that's a lot of green! These are available at local participating stores. Check with the store's customer service desk to see if they offer this benefit.

Value Items

Many of the shoppers I talk to firmly believe they'll save the most money by avoiding brand-name purchases. But if you buy items on sale and with a coupon, this isn't necessarily true, especially when the brand name is a value product.

Age-gender groups	Weekly cost	Monthly cost
	Thrifty plan	
Individuals		
Child:		
1 year	19.00	82.10
2-3 years	20.00	86.70
4-5 years	20.90	90.70
6-8 years	26.50	114.90
9-11 years	30.50	132.30
Male:		
12-13 years	32.30	139.90
14-18 years	33.50	145.00
19-50 years	35.80	155.20
51-70 years	32.70	141.90
71+ years	32.90	142.40
Female:		
12-13 years	32.20	139.50
14-18 years	32.00	138.70
19-50 years	32.20	139.70
51-70 years	31.80	137.60
71+ years	31.20	135.10
Families		
Family of 2:		
19-50 years	74.90	324.40
51-70 years	70.90	307.40
Family of 4:		
Couple, 19-50 years and children—		
2-3 and 4-5 years	109.00	472.40
6-8 and 9-11 years	125.10	542.10

For example, Dawn Ultra contains 30 percent more cleaning ingredients per drop than the leading nonconcentrated brand, unlike some larger bottles of dish liquid that have more water. With Dawn Ultra, you get what you pay for, more power, not more water. I especially like a value product like this because I can also clean more dishes without the water feeling greasy.

Another example of a value item is found in the critical area of paper products. Sometimes the cheaper versions end up costing you far more. For example, I usually buy Bounty paper towels because Bounty works hard to clean up spills using fewer sheets while saving me money. They are 25 percent thicker and clothlike, making it easier to handle all my cleaning messes, and they keep working for me—I just rinse, wring, and reopen to get tough jobs done.

Question: Will you take our cool grocery savings challenge? Look at the "Cost of Food at Home Chart" on pages 178–179 to calculate your family's current spending level. Then follow the previous grocery savings tips, and decide to reduce in at least one category or more to save _____ this next year!

Question: Will you calculate on the USDA food chart where you currently are in terms of thrifty, low-cost, moderate, or liberal? Then calculate how much you could save per year by moving to the next rank down.

Learn to Negotiate like an Apprentice

Anytime can be a good time to learn how to negotiate prices on the things you buy, but vacation is an especially good time. If you save money by paying less on consumer items, you could "earn" anywhere from $100 to $10,000 a year. It's just a matter of learning how to negotiate on everything from shoes to salaries. The key is to learn how to bargain without embarrassing yourself, your friends, or your family. Following are a few successful strategies to try.

- **Compare.** Furniture, phone plans, electronics, jewelry, and appliances are all highly negotiable. Find your desired item on a search robot such as Froogle.com, mySimon.com, Nextag.com, and eBay.com or in sale circulars from the Sunday paper. Then print out the price, take it into your store, and ask them to match it. Some stores, such as Wal-Mart, will automatically match competitors' ads (even on food items).

Blue Book of Online Savings

Shopping Robots

These help you find the best buy on the Internet for most items:

2save247.com	Ebates.com	Term4sale.com
Froogle.google.com	Jr.com	Esurance.com
Shopping.msn.com	Samsclub.com	Ehealthinsurance.com
Shopping.yahoo.com	Streetprices.com	**Travel**
Bizrate.com	Walmart.com	Jetblue.com
Consumerreports.org	**Entertainment**	Travelocity.com
Addall.com	Allenbrothers.com	Travelweb.com
mySimon.com	Couponpages.com	Travelzoo.com
Clothing	Entertainment.com	Expedia.com
Bluefly.com	Hotcoupons.com	Southwest.com
Eluxury.com	Deandeluca.com	Hotwire.com
eBay.com	Omahasteaks.com	Orbitz.com
Net-a-porter.com	Valpak.com	Priceline.com
Electronics	Vermontcountry	Sidestep.com
Shopper.cnet.com	store.com	Tripadvisor.com
Amazon.com	**Insurance**	**Used Books**
Bestbuy.com	1stquote.com	Abebooks.com
Buy.com	Instantquote.com	Alibris.com
Circuitcity.com	Itechusa.com	Amazon.com
Costco.com	Sbli.com	Barnesandnoble.com

- **Compensate.** If the salesperson cannot match the price, then ask for other freebies such as complimentary delivery, free accessories, or an extended warranty.
- **Continue.** If the salesperson grants extra perks, don't stop there. After you've secured these, ask for the manager, and ask her to match the competitor's price.
- **Clearance.** Look for clearance items in the store, especially when shopping for clothes, and ask the salesclerks to check the back for your size (not all clearance items are always out front). If they don't have your size, then ask a clerk to check another store, give you the sales price, and ship the item for free (more stores offer this service to compete with online retailers). I purchased six pairs of jeans for my kids with the original prices of $60 and sales prices of $20, saving $240!
- **Counter.** It never hurts to counter a price—if you ask for 20 percent off and they offer 10, then counter with 15 percent. When it comes to salary negotiations, you shouldn't accept the first offer. Most salaried professionals ask for 10 to 12 percent more than what they're offered and often settle for 7 to 8 percent more. If you did this with your first salary, it could add up to $500,000 by the time you're sixty years old!
- **Consider.** Don't limit the odds of success by asking for too much. The store has to make a profit. Small appliances are usually marked up 30 percent, while larger ones, such as washing machines, are marginalized by only 15 percent. However, most large furniture items and jewelry are increased by a whopping 100 percent!
- **Communicate.** Learn to say, "Is this your best price?" "Was this recently on sale, and can I have the sale price?" "Do you think you could ask your manager? I'll be happy to wait." "Hmm, this item

is a little damaged (makeup on the collar, an already-opened box, a ding or scratch). Could it be marked down?" And last but not least, "Thank you, I'll be back."

Shopping with Friends

Now that you've learned how to negotiate, you're ready to go shopping—again! But what about shopping with a friend? How do you still enjoy the process without becoming a miserly scrooge? On your next conquer-the-mall mission, try these tips for shopping and saving with a friend, because sometimes two can save more than one!

- **Clubbing.** Warehouse clubs like Sam's Club can be a great place to save—but not if you overspend to get quantity discounts. Buy these items with a friend, and each will take home half of the bounty with all of the savings. You can have an average "clubbing" savings of $10.

- **Perishables.** Produce is least expensive purchased in bulk. For example, a bushel of peaches or flat of strawberries costs less than "by the pound" purchases. Go in on these big buys together, and save even more. See an average "perishable" savings of $8.

- **New-card discounts.** If you (or a friend) want to open a store charge account for convenience, then do it on a day when you're shopping together. There is usually a "first day" discount that can range from 10 to 25 percent off all purchases—including clearance items. Pay your friend the cash immediately for your purchases, and encourage her to pay the charge account as soon as it arrives in the mail. But be careful about FICO scores—sometimes a new card isn't worth the discount. The new card discount is around $15.

- **Twofers.** Department stores often run "buy one item, get another item for a discount" sales. My friend Brenda and I bought a trendy shirt for $20 with the second one free—so we each paid only $10! Plus, you can eat lunch with a twofer lunch coupon found at Restaurant.com to save around $15 per person.

Know Your 123s of Online Savings

While you're online buying and selling at eBay, do some additional research to learn how to buy for less. You can cut some of your online purchase costs almost in half if you will simply try to layer the savings. Here are three steps to save big online:

1. The first step is to go to mySimon.com or Shopbot.com, both of which are shopping robots that will search the Internet for your item to find the best deal possible.

2. Once you've found the best deal, the second step is to go to a code site such as Dealhunting.com or Couponcabin.com to find the codes you need to save even more. Sometimes these codes are for free shipping, gifts, or discounts.

3. The final step is to get a rebate for your shopping by going to Ebates.com. If you have an account and get your friends to sign up under you, you can earn $5 per referral. Hundreds of online sites participate and will give you a rebate off your purchases. You'll get a check at the end of each month.

To avoid spam, be sure you deselect any offers made while signing up for a site. I also recommend that you use a throwaway e-mail address to sign up rather than giving your primary e-mail address.

Some of the best places to try out your new money-savings personality are online. But where do you go for different values? I learned about finding value back when I was in high school. Not only was I already a born saver, but I was a born entrepreneur and worked in my neighbor's car dealership in the office to earn money to fund my dreams. That's when I was first introduced to the *Kelley Blue Book* and discovered the wealth of information contained therein. It lists the wholesale, retail, and loan values of most cars! Well, there's a "blue book" for online buyers as well (see page 181); it will help you recession-proof your online purchases—no matter what your money personality.

Living Rich Questions

Will you take our cool grocery savings challenge? Look at the "Cost of Food at Home" chart in this chapter to figure your family's current spending level. Then follow the previous grocery savings tips, and decide to reduce in at least one category or more to save hundreds of dollars this next year!

Will you try to practice two suggestions from the "Learn to Negotiate like an Apprentice" section?

Will you buy one item this month using the three-step online savings plan?

10

Cruisin' to Vacation Savings

Travel, Entertain, and Eat Out Affordably

Where there are friends there is wealth.
TITUS MACCIUS PLAUTUS

It was the first night for formal dining on our Mexican cruise. There he was, my retired military man in full uniform, with pants that could still zip and pockets that didn't bulge at the seams! I was so proud of him as I stood proudly at his side, waiting for formal night aboard the cruise ship to start. As we chatted by the closed doors to the waiting room, Bob checked his new TAG Heuer watch, a present I had given him when his Stealth F-117 fighter jet was retired earlier in the month. Two warriors, a man and his jet, were now a part of history—but he still looked great in his uniform. I was about to tell him those thoughts one more time but was interrupted.

"Excuse me," a woman in a black jet beaded dress said to Bob. "Can you tell me how long it will be before the dining room doors open?"

Bob checked his TAG watch. "About three more minutes, ma'am."

She glided back to join her party, but scarcely had she left before an older gentleman with silver hair and a black Armani tux tapped his shoulder.

"Captain," he began, "my friends and I were discussing the average speed of a ship this size and wanted to know if you could tell us how fast your ship cruises."

Suddenly Bob and I both realized that some of these people thought

Eat Out More for Less

When recession hits, one of the first things people cut back on is eating out—but wait a minute! You don't have to be so drastic if you do it smart. Here are some ways to Cha Ching your entertainment and eating-out dollars.

- **Restaurants.** Want to try a new restaurant but don't want to pay full price? Go to Restaurant.com, a site that issues coupons and gift certificates for over 6,000 eateries around the country. Our family picks a spot and pays $10 for a $25 gift certificate—we save over 50 percent in the process. The average restaurant bill for a family of four is $86. Our family saves $43 x 52 weeks = $2,236.

- **Rich lunch, no dinner.** The average lunch costs anywhere from $3 to $15 less than the average dinner, and the portions may be more health friendly as well. If you want to go to the $50-an-entrée hot spot to celebrate your baby being potty trained, then opt for lunch and save $15 over the price of dinner. Lunching instead of dinnering saves an average of $9 per person x 2 (for a couple) = $18 savings per week x 52 weeks = $936 annual savings.

- **Rewards.** This option is recommended for those who eat out at least once a week because it requires a $49 annual registration fee. Go to the secure site at Rewardsnetwork.com and register your he was the ship's captain! In fact, when I saw the ship's captain later that night at dinner, I realized that Bob's uniform was more ornate, and his medals and ribbons made that poor captain look like a junior Cub Scout

credit or debit card to get up to 20 percent of the bill credited to your account when you eat at one of the 10,000 participating restaurants. Combine this savings with the previous tip, and you could be saving and/or banking up to 70 percent of your restaurant bill! Eating out once a week for a family of four—$86 per week at 20 percent savings x 52 weeks = $895.

- **Real savings.** Entertainment.com offers a coupon book that is available for 150 metro markets and costs between $25 and $45. Preview the coupon booklet for your area (or an area where you will vacation) to see if the coupons are ones you will use. An added benefit: you'll not only save on eating out, but you can also save on movie theaters, theme parks, dry cleaning, and at local shops. Average advertised total book savings—$17,000. To redeem only 25 percent is an annual savings of $4,250.

- **Reaping even more.** Check the Sunday paper or weekday paper for local restaurant values. The Sunday FSIs (free-standing inserts) have chain restaurant coupons, and the weekday paper may alert you to special days when an eatery offers buy one, get one free meals, kids eat free, or early bird specials. Average FSI savings is 25 percent for a family of four, or a total of $15 per fast food dinner. This savings x 52 weeks = $780.

compared to my guy! The rest of the night I enjoyed watching the attention my retired fighter pilot got as passengers asked him various questions about the ship. He still had it!

It was great to go on vacation and enjoy the benefits of a shipshape ship and a shipshape spouse too. The best part was the price: only $199 per person! (That is not a misprint.) Many families feel that with news of a recession, they can no longer enjoy vacations because they just can't afford one in today's uncertain economy. But if you believe that, then you are just as confused as those passengers who looked at my husband as the ship's captain—you are suffering from a case of mistaken identity. Your vacation doesn't have to go undercover or disappear; you just need to know how to dress it up a bit so you can afford to go out. Whether you want to go on a cruise, eat out with your family, or just have the freedom to shop with a girlfriend, you *can* still have fun and recession-proof your life. Here are some tips that allow you to have it all and still stay on budget for your vacation.

Question: Are you willing to try paying cash for your next vacation?

Saving Money on Vacations

Too many families have trouble in an uncertain economy because they charge their vacations, thereby getting further in debt. Or they forgo a vacation altogether, which isn't very much fun, baby! An impending recession does not mean you have to stop taking vacations. Sometimes it just means learning to think of them in a more creative way.

The $199 Cruise: Fact or Fiction?

These cruises are readily available but are sometimes deceptive. First, you have to find them, and then you need to use savvy and simple techniques to keep them from costing too much. Here are some ways to make the $199 cruise factual and keep it from becoming fiction once you're onboard.

Top Ten Tips for Titanic Savings

1. Travelzoo. The first step is to subscribe to the "Top Twenty" weekly travel deals on Travelzoo.com, and be prepared to act fast once you get notification of the $199 cruise. We have also taken advantage of their deals in order to have a sweet experience in Ireland ($1,199 covered two round-trip tickets, five nights at B and Bs, and a rental car), and "honey time" in Hawaii ($799 covered airfare for two and five nights on Waikiki Beach).

2. Relocation cruises. If you don't want to sit and wait for the "Top Twenty," then do your own research (Google "$199 Cruises" and "Relocation Cruises"). The latter are special deals when a ship is being taken to a different port for a new assignment. For example, if the ship is relocating from the U.S. to Europe to be put into service for a Mediterranean cruise, it will take passengers for the ten-day journey and then you fly home. The rub is that you'll pay more than $199, and you'll usually pay a one-way ticket as well, but there are fabulous deals to be had.

3. Just say no. This little tip will save you hundreds of bucks. Closely evaluate all the specials offered on ship. You might as well call these specials "moneymakers for the cruise line"; they offer art, jewelry, alcohol, and spa services as soon as you get onboard. For example, you can sign up the first day for spa specials, but is it really a good deal to have a $239 stone massage for only $199? No. Instead, I chose the $99 Ladies Night Out special, where I got five fifteen-minute spa services (a facial, massage, and hair treatment). Say no to spa extras, special drinks, jewelry (which will likely be on sale for 50 percent off the last day of the cruise), photos, and more.

4. Spa tips. Be prepared to say no when you go to the spa on that $99 special (or the equivalent) because they make most of their

money on the products they try to sell you. It's pretty amazing—
the staff starts to "sell" while they're massaging your shoulders or
finishing up your beautiful hair, while you're relaxed and vulnera-
ble. Then they start to tell you how your hair is really in bad
shape or your muscles need a special oil. Too often, staff have
convinced me that I desperately needed $212 worth of hair treat-
ments and body lotions or my hair would fall out and my back
would stiffen up. Thank goodness I came to my senses at the
register when I saw the total in black and white. You'll learn
that most staff is required to pitch products. You can avoid the
hard sell by saying something like, "You know, if you don't mind,
I'd like to just relax in silence awhile. I need the space." They'll
understand, and you'll walk away with the relaxing knowledge of
savvy savings.

5. Pass on the soda pass. The first day you may be offered a "soda
   pass" that gives you all the pop you can drink for one low price.
   Au contraire! You want to drink lots of *water, not soda,* on this
   cruise to get your money's worth. Water keeps you hydrated after
   all the salt in that rich food. Plus, you might feel obligated to
   drink your weight in soda if you buy a pass, and the end result
   will be an unhealthy feeling (even with diet soda!). The goal isn't
   to leave the cruise feeling bloated and stressed but healthy and
   relaxed instead.

6. Pack two water bottles. Each person should pack two bottles of
   water (we stick them in shoes in our luggage) to save big bucks.
   You cannot bring in cases of water or six-packs of soda. That's
   generally not allowed. Water onboard sells for $2.50 to $4.00 per
   bottle, and it also costs that much onshore too. But you can bring
   a couple of bottles to use and refill. The tap water in your room
   comes from the same water source used for glasses of water in the

dining room. Keep and refill your bottles to save on the cost of having to buy new bottles at ports of call and while on excursions.

7. Digital pix. One of my fave nights is formal night, and photos are a must. By all means take pictures from the ship's service. You can look at them later and don't have to buy them. But be sure to have your new friends onboard take plenty of digital pictures with your own camera—you'll save the cost of the formal photo and probably get better shots anyway.

8. Rank and research shore excursions. You could easily double or triple the bottom-line total for your cruise by spending money on shore excursions. Before you sail, when you go to the cruise Web site to print your boarding pass, look at the shore excursions and print out the options. Or do this as soon as you get onboard. You and your sailing mate (spouse, friend, mom) should rank the excursions. The first step is to pick the ones you **like best** for each port. Each person should pick his or her top three for each port of call, giving a number three to your top pick, two for the second best, and one for your last choice. Give the same ranking for the excursion with the **most time** (for example, a five-hour island tour): three for the most time, two for the second most, one for the least amount of time. Finally, rank the **cost** of each: three for the least expensive, two for the next expensive, and one for the most money. Add up all of these points, and the excursion with the biggest number is usually the best value.

9. Excursion extras. It's important to walk and work off some of that rich food. You'll feel better and get more for your money, time, and effort. Try to walk as much as possible on excursions to avoid bus, shuttle, or cab fares. Bring your own water bottles (see tip 6), and don't throw away the bottle when you're done. Eat breakfast onboard before you go to save money on food. Try to postpone

lunch until you're back on the ship, or bring an apple or banana
to tide you over (we order room service the night before a port of
call and have these delivered to our room). If the port is close to
the town, you can even walk back onboard (getting that coveted
exercise) and eat lunch, then go back out again.

10. It's show business. The entertainment onboard is generally pretty
good, but it can be hit-and-miss. Get your money's worth by
going to the shows (and walk out if the show stinks—plenty of
people do that when it's not worth your time or the entertainer is
offensive). Sign up for free classes like salsa, line dancing, Pilates,
or yoga, and try your hand at karaoke. Do these with your new
shipmates to multiply the fun. It's all part of the cruise experience!

Cruises are great, but they may not be practical for your family right
now. There are a lot of creative ways to have a great vacation through planning, research, and readjusting expectations. It's best to get the entire family involved, as it paves the way for greater satisfaction as well as savings.

Family Meetings

One of the tips we've found to be the most lucrative when it comes to paying cash for a vacation is to get the entire family to buy in to the trip. Consider having a family meeting full of give and take. Be prepared to
compromise as to where you go. Let the "team members" understand that
no one will get all of what they want, but everyone will get a little of what
they want. Have family members write down where they want to go, what
they want to do, how long they want to stay, and rank their vacation
"wants" from one to three. Then ask them how much they think their
dream vacation will cost. Have a computer handy, and calculate how much
the going rate at Expedia.com or Orbitz.com is for their dream vacation;
then let them know the family's cash budget for the vacation.

Have these meetings once a week, and make it fun by ordering pizza or meeting at breakfast with doughnuts. Set the timer for an hour, have paper and pen ready, create an agenda, and discuss only that topic until the timer rings. Then revisit the discussion next week until the details are established. It's best to start these meetings six months before the desired vacation time. It may seem awkward (or futile) in the early meetings, but stick with it. Eventually you'll have ownership by all your family members, and they will each have a budget for souvenirs, excursions, special events, and even food. Not only will it keep your costs on budget, it is also a fun way to teach kids the value of a dollar and how they can live within their means.

Twice the Fun at Half the Price

If you have friends you like *a lot* and you think your friendship can survive the test of a family vacation, then double up with that family and cut your bills in half. The Greaves family did this with the Morton family and enjoyed it so much that they made it an every-other-year tradition.

The normal price of a weeklong mountain cabin rental with three bedrooms was $1,900. "We made sure we knew all the costs ahead of time and that there were no financial surprises," says Loretta Greaves. Each family paid $800 and their own gas for a destination that might not have been available to them otherwise.

"We couldn't really swing nearly $2,500 for the week on my pastor salary, but we could afford half that amount and go half on the meals. We've truly enjoyed our time off," said Mike Morton.

You don't have to rent a cabin to double up with another family. Many different kinds of rentals can be found at Findrental.com. Suite hotels that offer extra rooms are also an option, such as the ones found at Orbitz.com or Cheaphotels.com. For those who love the great outdoors, sharing campsite fees or RV rentals can split the price of a camping adventure. At

RVrental.com we found rentals across the country that ranged from $117 to $385 per day. Depending on the owner of the RV, other charges to consider are hospitality kits, kitchen kits, and emergency road kits. Cleaning fees will apply if the RV is not returned in the condition in which it was rented.

Save on Airfare

There's no reason to pay full price on airfare when so many online options will help you get the best price. If you want to go to one central site that will check all the other sites' search engines, go to Bookingbuddy.com. They have proven that they can save the average customer $100 per ticket, as their engines will use the search engines for dozens of other sites such as Travelocity.com, Expedia.com, Priceline.com, Orbitz.com, and Cheap tickets.com. When you find the best price, you can book directly on that site with a link from Bookingbuddies.com. For instance, a family of four can save an average of $100 per ticket per person.

Don't forget about the timing when you buy those tickets. The best day of the week to buy is usually Wednesday. Peter Greenberg of Fodor.com says that this is the best day to buy airline tickets, and the reason is thanks to small, upstart airlines.[1] In the airline business, the weakest competitors usually begin fare wars, while the bigger airlines tend to raise fares. Fridays are when these new fare wars usually begin.

When airline A decides to raise fares, it usually happens late in the day on Friday. By Saturday, airline A's major competitors will probably match that fare increase (that's why you should never book your tickets over a weekend). But what if the major competitors do not match the higher fares? Then airline A drops their fares again by late Sunday or Monday.

On the other hand, let's say that the fare war is going in the downside direction. Airline B decides to lower fares, and it happens late on a Friday. By Saturday and Sunday, the other major airlines may lower their fares to compete. On Monday, they are seeing how the new fares do in the marketplace. By Tuesday, if the fares are doing well (meaning lots of sales), then airline C might jump into the fray with an even lower fare. Prices may go even lower by Wednesday, and that's the day to buy!

By Thursday the fare wars and sales are usually over, and it begins all over again on Friday. The best time of the day on Wednesday is 1:00 a.m. (set the alarm), which is an hour past Tuesday and an hour past midnight, when most airlines usually reload their computers with the newest fares.

A Purpose-Driven Vacation

Mac and Dina Thompson first discovered their favorite family vacation spot when they had an ample budget for family fun. They went to a private campground in Colorado and fell in love with the staff, landscape, and activities. They also caught the vision of how combining volunteering with vacationing could help teach their kids the concept of servant missions.

Instead of paying $1,000 for the week, they had a working vacation for free.

Not all campgrounds offer this kind of a trade-off, but if your family enjoys this kind of environment, it would be worth your time to contact a local retreat center or campground. Go to Acacamps.org for the American Camp Association to find a location near you.

Elderhostel.org offers those fifty-five and older up to 10,000 learning vacation options starting at as little as $556 for a six-day photography workshop in Massachusetts.

Wilderness Volunteers (Wildernessvolunteers.org) is a nonprofit organization created in 1997 that offers people of any age a chance to help and maintain national parks, forests, and wilderness areas across the United States. Everything from trail maintenance to revegetation projects are on the agenda. Participants provide their own camping gear and share campsite chores. Most Wilderness Volunteer trips last about a week and cost around $219.

Couple-Time Savings

An average date of dinner and a movie costs $80, but the "free" dates listed below save $80 per night. If you want to live rich for less, it's important to look at various ways that vacations go hand in hand with entertainment. The household entertainment budget takes a lot of different forms, but it's always in good form to make time for your honey. Whether you're on vacation in another land or at home and wanting to have a fun date, here are some nearly free ways to have quality time with your mate while keeping costs low.

- **Beach time.** When playing in the waves, take time to snuggle your mate in the water.
- **Balcony dates.** Try to select a room with a view, and while the kids are asleep or watching a movie, have coffee on the veranda under the stars.
- **Flowers, anyone?** Surprise your mate with a bouquet from a street vendor.
- **Sunsets**. Check out the time of sunset at Weather.com, and then schedule dinner at a local restaurant, asking for a table with a view.
- **Gifts.** Before your vacation, wrap a few inexpensive yet meaningful gifts for your mate. Place one on his or her pillow each night.
- **Touch.** Meaningful touch can often get lost in the rapid pace of life. Grab your spouse's hand, and give him or her a kiss under the moonlight.

- **Carriage ride.** Take advantage of the romantic element in family activities. Let your kids ride in the front of the carriage while you snuggle in the back.
- **Reflection time.** Schedule a date at the end of each day to share what you felt was your most romantic moment and why—you may be surprised at what you learn about your mate in the process!

Living Rich Questions

Will you try a family meeting to plan the financial portion of your vacation?

Are you willing to try paying cash for your next vacation?

Will you try two "eating out for less" options in the next month and track your savings?

11

Bubble, Bubble, Toil, and Trouble

Attain and Maintain the Home of Your Dreams

He does not posses wealth that

allows it to possess him.

BENJAMIN FRANKLIN

It was early in the morning, and I was getting ready to take my dogs for a walk. A strange fog lingered outside, and I got the creepy feeling that something was terribly wrong in our neighborhood. There had been rumors going around about one of the neighbors, and I looked over at the house, wondering if they were true.

I noticed an odd light coming from the garage and heard strange, high-pitched laughter. I got the odd sense that the gossip might in fact be true.

I could be living next door to a witch.

My dog Buddy broke loose from his leash to check out the front yard. The alleged witch, dressed in black, emerged from the garage and began walking her trash can to the curb.

Well, Buddy obviously found it creepy as well because he started to bark at her for walking down our driveway (it's actually a shared driveway, but he sees them as one). After about five seconds of this, I caught up with Buddy, took his leash, and began to walk away.

That's when I heard the laughter.

I turned to see the creature, her face angry, yelling something at us.

Now, I try to be a kind and courteous person to all people. Even witches. So I turned, walked back a few feet, and asked, "What?"

The hag shrieked a noise that I'm sure was designed to turn me to stone. Aha! She didn't know I was half deaf and remained untouched by her powers. She yelled—I kid you not—"I said, if your dog barks at me again, I'll sue you and your little dog too."

I was shocked. Yes, we did live in California, which some call the "sue you state." But *no one* had ever threatened to sue my dog. I thought she'd probably cook him up in a stew. Then I decided that the modern witch stews, then sues. And I walked away.

Suddenly, a black car drove up to the door, and two bankers emerged and presented the witch with a bubble of trouble. It was the same bubble that trapped thousands of investors in the dotcom crash a few years ago. The California housing bubble had made the witch's house go bust. She made the mistake of buying an ARM, an adjustable rate mortgage. It adjusted so much with rising interest rates that she couldn't pay her mortgage. Cold water was thrown on her dream house.

She melted.

Oh...my...pretty...

And then I woke up!

I couldn't believe I'd had such a vivid dream about my neighbor. I lived next door to an empty house. Yes, the bank owned it. But the previous occupant was not green! I think my dreams were a combination of reading too much material in research for this chapter, a very spicy pizza, and dogs barking waaay too early in the morning!

Avoid Neglect and Save Big

Exterior Item to Be Checked	Neglect Cost
Roof: Visually check shingles from ground. Watch for missing shingles or broken pieces. Check gutters and downspouts. Check every six months.	Water Damage: $5,000.
Gutters and downspouts: Check and remove any debris to assure unobstructed water flow away from foundation. Check every six months.	Foundation Damage: $10,000.
Veneer or siding: With brick, watch for deteriorating bricks or masonry. For siding, watch for warping or rot. Check all painted surfaces. Check every six months.	Rot Damage: $3,000.
Windows and doors: Check caulking around doors and windows, glazing around windowpanes. Check every six months.	Energy Loss: $600.
Lawn and garden: Watch for accumulation of tree limbs, branches, and debris that can attract wood eating insects. Check every three months.	See Termite Damage Below.
Asphalt driveways: Check for cracks or deterioration. Reseal if necessary. Check every six months.	Professional Driveway Repairs: $11,000.
Heating and cooling: Make sure outside unit is unobstructed. Clean unit with garden hose. Check every six months.	Repair Damage Caused by Obstruction: $1,000.

Interior Item to Be Checked	Neglect Cost
Attic: Examine for evidence of any leaks. Check every three months.	Water Damage: $5,000.
Baths: Check for evidence of any leaks, especially around toilets and under sinks (vinyl tile will usually discolor if water is getting underneath it). Check grout on ceramic tile. Check monthly.	New Flooring, Water Rot: $5,000.
Kitchen: Check for leaks under sink and around dishwasher. Check burner operation on stove. Check grout on any ceramic tile. Check monthly.	New Cabinets or Flooring: $3,000.
Kitchen: Clean dust from refrigerator condenser (rear of unit). Check every three months	New Compressor: $600.
Heating System: Change filter; check coils for buildup. Check monthly.	Energy Loss: $300.
Water Heater: Check for signs of leaks. Check monthly.	Water Damage: $3,000.
Water Heater: Drain to remove any sediment. In areas with hard water, drain every three months. Check every six months.	Energy Loss: $200.
Smoke Detectors: Check operation. Check monthly.	Partial Fire Damage: $50,000.
Smoke Detectors: Change batteries. Check every six months.	Deductible for Fire Damage: $5,000.
Basement or crawl space: Check for cracks or any sign of dampness or leaks. Check for any evidence of termites or wood eating insects. Check every six months.	Termite Damage: $20,000.

As I worked on this chapter, I thought of the first time Bob and I walked into the first home we would own as a couple. We had lived in base housing with all our kids for a dozen years while digging out of debt and building for the future. Our friends, Fred and Cheryl, owned this gorgeous home in Alamogordo, and we walked into their house to have dinner with them one night. The house wasn't for sale, and we weren't in the market.

Later that night, Bob said, "Wow, the Zeitzes have a beautiful home, don't they? I wonder if we'll ever own a home like that."

We moved to New York for another assignment, and then Bob got a job flying the F-117 Stealth fighter back in Alamogordo again. As it turns out, the Zeitzes were moving to another state and asked us if we wanted to buy their house. Because we'd followed the ideas I share in this chapter, we were in a position to buy a dream home and live in it with comfortable monthly payments. Dreams do come true, if you are wise and strategic and then throw in a little diligence to make them happen.

These days it's not only about buying a home; it's also about *keeping* that home during difficult economic times. The strategies in this chapter will give you steps to help you get into the right dwelling for the right price and keep costs down so you can hold on to your home.

Five Mortgage Pluses and Minuses

Some Mortgage Plus Actions

- **Make on-time debt payments.** Every thirty-, sixty-, or ninety-day delinquency on a loan or credit card is going to reduce the credit score on your report. This is a consideration a loan officer will have to take into account when approving your mortgage and the amount of the loan. If it appears that you have trouble making debt payments on time, the lender will be very hesitant to loan you money.

- **If you have to miss a payment, carefully choose which one.** If you find yourself the victim of downsizing and can't pay a bill for a few months, you might have to miss a loan payment of some kind. Be strategic in choosing that missed payment. You should miss the credit card payment first, followed by the payment on any installment loan you might have, and finally the payment for an existing mortgage. A missed mortgage payment will have the greatest impact on your credit score and will also impact your ability to get a good home loan in the future, which is why it is important to be strategic in the monthly payment you might have to miss. A missed credit card payment will not have as great an impact as a missed car payment.

- **Pay off debt.** It's important to pay off as many smaller debts as you can so you'll have a better chance at getting a good mortgage rate. Even if you end up putting down a smaller amount at closing and have a larger mortgage, you'll be better off than paying the high interest rates of most consumer debt. Paying off debt improves your credit score while releasing more disposable income at the same time. It's a very good two-for-one benefit if I've ever seen one!

- **Mortgage takes priority.** If you or your spouse has a new job and the means to secure multiple loans (such as a mortgage, auto loan, and new credit cards), secure the mortgage loan first. Whenever your credit is scored, each application for credit becomes a liability to your rating. Numerous credit inquiries can hurt your overall credit score, especially if they are filed in the months prior to the mortgage loan review process. When you secure your mortgage loan before you buy a new car or furniture, then you've maximized your credit rating while it is at its highest number, and this will add up to a lower interest rate and a lower monthly house payment.

- **Save, save, save.** It's best to increase the size of the down payment you're able to make by saving as much as possible. Invest the money you are saving in secure accounts that offer reasonable rates

of return such as Ingdirect.com. Start a savings strategy that will
allow you to put more toward this goal by taking your coffee in a
travel mug every day instead of stopping at Starbucks, which can
save over $20 a week. Or bring a microwavable meal for lunch at
work and your own water bottle instead of going out for a burger
in order to save another $25 a week. Or implement any of the
dozens of money savings ideas in this book to become truly proactive in your goal of home ownership.

Mortgage Minuses—Avoid These

- **Making big purchases.** If you have to get a loan for a large purchase, such as a $15,000 auto loan, it could prevent you from
  qualifying for the mortgage amount you want—don't do this
  before you request a mortgage loan. Lenders do not look favorably
  upon adding debt upon debt. Besides that, the more money you
  are spending on loans, the less you will have to put toward a
  mortgage.

- **Living beyond your means.** If you try to obtain a loan that
  would raise your payments from $500 in rent to a whopping
  $1,600 per month for principal, interest, and insurance, then you
  are likely to experience what the industry calls "payment shock."
  You don't want to live beyond your means. A lender will look at
  this differential, and you will find yourself in one of two situations:
  (1) you won't qualify for the loan, or (2) you will end up having to
  cover too much loan with too little money.

- **Prequalified versus preapproved.** When you are *prequalified* for a
  loan, you are basically given an estimate of how much you will
  qualify for after you've submitted income, credit, and debt information. In this case, the lender does not pull credit reports, check
  debt-to-income ratios, or perform other underwriting steps. But

by getting *preapproved,* these latter steps are performed, and you are that much closer to obtaining a loan and locking in a rate and term. The first is an estimate; the latter is much closer to the final product.

- **Money personalities.** In an earlier chapter we saw that everyone has a different kind of money personality—some are born spenders and others are born savers. Don't forget this when it comes to getting a mortgage loan. If you take out a thirty-year fixed-rate loan rather than a fifteen-year mortgage and invest the money saved on monthly payments, you might earn a higher return on your money in the long run. But few money personalities have this kind of discipline. If you're the kind of personality that spends any extra money you have, it would be better to get the shorter term, which will force you to invest your money toward paying off your house in a shorter amount of time.

- **Adding hidden burdens.** Don't forget the extras involved in home ownership. You will have to cover short-term and long-term repairs and maintenance: When something breaks you will have to pay to have it repaired or replaced. On the financial side of the equation, don't forget that home ownership brings the additional responsibility of greater financial accountability.

Are You Paying Too Much for Mortgage Fees?

When you shop for a house, you expect to negotiate on the price, but most people don't realize that you should also shop around for a mortgage broker and negotiate the interest rate as well as associated fees. Let prospective lenders know that you have other options for who will provide your mortgage and that you will go with the company that provides the most attractive package—with the lowest interest rate and minimal fees.

After you already know the pluses and minuses of mortgages, consider the fact that overcharges for mortgage fees are more common than ever. A new study finds that dubious fees may mean that consumers are overpaying to get a mortgage, according to data collected from more than 10,000 recent borrowers by the National Mortgage Complaint Center, a watchdog organization that helps consumers avoid overcharges. Here are the most common mortgage overages and how to avoid them:

- **Inflated credit report and courier fees.** Some lenders are charging up to $65 for pulling your credit report. That's unusually high considering the fact that credit reporting bureaus only charge $6 to $18 per report. Using the same tactics, some lenders charge as much as $100 for courier fees for shipping your closing documents, while the majority of overnight express services charge only $22. These methods are not illegal or even unethical; they are simply ways lenders seek to pad the fees in order to increase their profit margin. It's very similar to buying stamps from a privately owned mail service provider at a 20 percent markup. When you buy directly from the post office, you don't have to pay padded fees. You don't want to pay superfluous fees for credit reporting and courier services either. Research the going prices on these services by going to Fedex.com or Ups.com as well as Creditexpert.com, print out the prices, and tell your lender up front that you refuse to pay any more than the going rate for these services.
- **Document prep and administration fees.** The origination fee should include these services, so don't pay them! Ask your lender to waive these fees.
- **Yield spread premiums.** Lenders increase your interest rate slightly to include origination and other fees so you don't have to pay them out of pocket at closing. But some lenders and mortgage

brokers double-dip by charging both the fees and the higher interest rate. While you are still in the "shopping" phase for a mortgage provider, ask your broker directly if their firm charges a "yield spread premium"; if so, confirm with them in writing that you shouldn't pay any additional fees. If you define these terms up front, you shouldn't run into the later problem of duplicate fees. If a broker indicates that they will charge both the yield spread premium and origination and other fees, let them know it is an unacceptable offer and that you are shopping around for a lender who won't charge double fees. With the current squeeze on mortgage providers, it has become more of a buyer's market, and you are in the driver's seat to be able to ask for equitable provisions to your loan that will allow you to keep more of your own money at closing time.

- **Padded title insurance fees.** When you are shopping for lenders, look for all of the above as well as watching for those who don't tack on a lot of extra charges for services such as title search and document preparation. These can add hundreds of dollars to your closing costs and should be included in the price of title insurance, which, depending on where you live, can be as high as $6,000.

Tips for Buying and Selling, Downsizing, or Upgrading

Housing is the largest line item on the family budget, and a huge recession may mean a huge decision: Do you drop some serious debt, or do you consider downsizing?

Before you take such a drastic approach to budget-cutting, give the following housing-savvy measures a try, and see how well they add up to long-term safety for your mortgage and home.

Homeowner's Checklist

To get the most out of your home financially, both now and in the future, it's important to keep a close eye on some specific items.

- **Information.** Keep a copy of the following in your files and in a safety deposit box: property address, legal description, date of purchase, and previous owner. You should also have current addresses and account or policy numbers on the following: real estate agent, closing agent, title company, insurance company and agent, and the mortgage company—and any and all policy numbers.

- **Identity theft.** Your credit rating greatly impacts your ability to trade up on a home in the future. In order to maintain your good credit rating and catch possible identity theft, get a regular copy of your credit report. Go to Freecreditreport.com for a free copy. You can also remember the basics of never giving out social security numbers without proper assurances that the recipient is a valid source. If you get an e-mail from a bank or credit card company asking you to update your information, never select the link provided in the e-mail. Instead, call the phone number on the back of your card or found on your monthly statement, or go to their Web site directly. Shred all credit card applications you get in the mail, and when you eventually discard outdated credit card bills, shred them too!

- **Inventory.** Take an inventory of the valuables in your home, and update it on a regular basis. Periodically, you may need to take photos and upgrade coverage on the insurance policy. Go to Ourfamilyplace.com for suggested inventory pages.

- **Insurance.** As a former insurance agent, I was able to almost double the size of the clientele for the agency I worked for by doing some simple research. I would find out what people were currently paying for their homeowner's policies and help them find a cheaper rate. Most of these policies are paid through the mortgage company's escrow account. You can save a lot by getting a new quote at renewal time each year. To get started, go to Freeinsurance quotes.com or Insweb.com.

- **Inexpensive safety.** There are some basic and inexpensive security measures that equip every house for safety and keep you from losing thousands...and sometimes everything: Deadbolt locks cost just $20 to $45, motion detector security lights are $20 to $60, window locks are $5 to $10, smoke detectors are $8 to $35, carbon monoxide detectors are $35 to $75, and fire extinguishers are just $20 to $60.

- **Interest rates.** The rule of thumb for a good value on refinancing your home is that you should plan on being in the home for at least another three years, and the fixed (not variable) interest rate should be a minimum of two full points lower than what you are currently paying. Here's an example of a thirty-year mortgage originally financed at 9.25 percent APR and with twenty-three years remaining on the loan, compared with a refinance for fifteen years at 7.25 percent APR. Original finance amount was $100,000, and the balance is $93,808.

Original Loan		Refinanced Loan	
Mortgage Amount	$100,000	Mortgage Amount	$93,808
Monthly	$823	Monthly	$856
Payments Left	276	Payments Left	180
Total of Remaining Payments	$227,148	Total of Remaining Payments	$154,080

- **Instant HELOCs.** A home equity line of credit is similar to your banker selling you a gun and teaching you how to pull the trigger to shoot yourself in the foot. That's what happens when a HELOC credit card is secured. The credit companies tout it as "a convenient way to access your home's equity without refinancing your mortgage every time you need money." Yeah, right. When they say "convenient," think Burger King convenient. The credit card promo reads: "Your credit is available 24 hours a day for everyday purchases like gas, groceries, and clothes or whenever you need cash. NowLine can be used at millions of locations world-wide, anywhere Visa is accepted." Now if a family is truly hard up for cash and is faced with the awful choice of paying for life's daily expenses by credit card or using a HELOC, one could argue that a HELOC is the better option because it's the least expensive in the short term. That's because HELOCs, which are tied to the prime rate, carry lower rates than credit cards, and the interest is typically tax deductible. But for a bank to suggest in its promos that HELOCs are a fine way to pay for dinner? I think that's shocking. A HELOC credit card should be avoided unless your family is unemployed or on the verge of losing your car or home. It's just another way to borrow on your future in order to live for today. It's also another way to incur more debt, and it will keep you from paying off your home that much sooner.
- **Improvement list.** It's important to keep a list of all improvements on your home—from a new air conditioner to a water heater. It can help you now (on your taxes) and later (when you sell your home). Also, capital gains taxes will be based on the difference between the sales price (less any selling expenses) minus the adjusted basis. You should check with your tax advisor each year, but the IRS usually defines improvements as those items that "add

to the value of your home, prolong its useful life, or adapt it to new uses." You can add improvements to the basis of the value of your property, but be sure to keep meticulous records of these expenses. Examples include putting a recreation room in your unfinished basement, adding another bathroom or bedroom, putting up a fence, installing new plumbing or wiring, getting a new roof, or paving your driveway.

- **Inspections.** It can be very alarming and costly to discover that your home has some kind of pest infestation. Not only will you have to pay the expense of debugging your home, but there may be the added expense of repairing structural damage. Have a pest control professional inspect your home on a regular basis.

- **Involvement in taxes.** When is the last time you thought of reviewing your real estate taxes? I recently spoke with our local county tax assessor, and he said that very few people dispute their tax assessment, but there are times when it's important to do so. Unless your situation is an obvious oversight that the assessor agrees with, you will need to be prepared to back up your claim regarding your property value. This could include an appraisal or a comparative market analysis. The comparative market analysis will document recorded sales of houses similar to yours, and these services are sometimes offered free by real estate agents. However, the assessment by a real estate agent is not the same as a legal document provided by a licensed appraiser.

There's an old saying that an ounce of prevention is worth a pound of cure. There is a lot you can do to prevent unneeded and untimely expenses. We've also listed on page 203 the Cha Ching "neglect cost" that the lack of preventive maintenance can run versus repairing the item once it progresses beyond nominal repairs. Please note that the neglect cost mentioned is on the extreme low end of such repairs.

Living Rich Questions

What "mortgage plus" actions can you take today that will help you secure a better mortgage next time you buy a home or refinance?

Are you paying too much for mortgage fees?

Will you go through the homeowner's checklist and see where you stack up?

12

The 10/10/80 Legacy

Living Rich in the Ways That Matter Most

Content makes poor men rich
and discontent makes rich men poor.
BENJAMIN FRANKLIN

A man with a knife in his hand shouts, "The flux capacitor is…"

His adoring followers respond, "Fluxing!" as cheers go up from the crowd.

The man takes his knife and begins to sharpen the end of a stick into a fine point.

"Hello. My name is Inigo Montoya. You killed my father, prepare to…"

"Die!" the crowd shouts in hearty reply.

Finally the man puts a marshmallow on the stick, holds it over the campfire, and says, "We're men! We're men in tights!"

He hears the response. "We roam around the forest, looking for fights!"

He purposefully picks up a graham cracker. "You're killing me, Smalls!… First you take the graham. You stick the chocolate on the graham. Then you roast the mallow. When the mallow's flaming, you stick it on the chocolate. Then you cover it with the other end. Then…"

The kids yell, "YOU SCARF!"

"And when I eat s'mores, I like to say, 'Go ahead, punk...' "

They all shout: "Make my day!"

No, this is not a secret meeting of the deranged and demented. It's our family sitting around the campfire, shouting lines from our favorite movies in succinct order. (The above quotes are from *Back to the Future; The Princess Bride; Robin Hood: Men in Tights; The Sandlot;* and *Sudden Impact.*) It's one of those family traditions that makes forever memories; these camping memories are some of my personal favorites. We still camp every summer with our school-aged children and the kids who come home from college. I often reflect on the treasures these kids are to us.

For half of my marriage and most of their lives, I've been an author and speaker. As the responsibilities in my work have increased, so have the benefits. I've taken each of the kids on special trips related to my work: to New York City and Broadway, to downtown Chicago and the famous Navy Pier, to historic downtown Fort Worth and the Will Rogers Coliseum, and even to Bismarck, North Dakota and the Space Aliens Grill and Bar. Yes, there have been perks for my kids as a result of the strange and wonderful world of writing and speaking.

Throughout the years, I've heard one comment over and again: How do you do it all?

Truthfully, I don't.

I've made it a habit to travel only twice a month—max.

I turn down projects because of the time involved.

In order to leave the kind of legacy I want to leave my kids, I say no to a lot of good things to leave room for what is best—time with them.

Nothing means more to me than my family. Our kids are the greatest treasures Bob and I have. They are our most valuable assets. They make us rich. They will leave their kids a legacy, I believe, of silly songs around the campfire, classic movies about men in tights, and a true knowledge that the best way to handle your money is to give away that first 10 percent, save the next 10 percent, and live wisely and well on the final 80 percent.

I believe they'll know how to live below their means and have rich lives. But it won't stop there. Because of the 10/10/80 Rule, they'll invest in their communities. There will be third-world children and underprivileged people that they financially support. Schools in poor villages will be funded, wells for drinking water will be dug, and rice fields will be purchased to provide a living for poor villagers.

What Is Your Legacy?

You'll leave some kind of a financial legacy too, either good or bad. A ripple effect of good can be a part of the legacy we leave behind—thousands, if not millions, of people can be positively affected by responsible giving. Lives will be saved and new legacies started…

Or you can leave a legacy of debt. In fact, from what I've observed with current debt trends, the youngest baby boomers may leave their kids zero assets and zero cash, and no money to fund worthy nonprofit organizations.

When our country was founded, people like Benjamin Franklin spread a practical gospel of hard work, temperance, and frugality. Most early Americans embraced that philosophy, and the result was incredible. The United States has been a wealthy nation from its founding, and as a whole, it was not corrupted by this affluence. Up until the fifties, our country remained productive, prudent, and purposed. Our society encouraged and valued spending what you earned and didn't celebrate debt and financial decadence.

But in the last forty years, we have changed with the advent of easy credit, irresponsible spending, and a general lack of contentment. Between 1989 and 2001, credit debt nearly tripled from $238 billion to $692 billion. Last year it was up to $937 billion.

The result of the current American financial culture is that lives are being ravished by debt and families destroyed. My desire is to help these families learn how to get out of financial bondage and stay free. Every day, more people are learning that living rich means living responsibly and well.

When Bob and I first got married, we didn't have much and learned the hard lesson of being content with what we had. Our debt load from a previous life of indulgence and divorce had cured us of the materialism that comes with easy credit. We had seen the kind of senseless materialism that motivated the greedy to nonchalantly go through money and marriages as if they were changing underwear. We didn't want that for ourselves or for our kids. The true wealth we possess, the assets that make us eternally rich, are peace of mind, freedom from money worries, and wanting what we have in terms of material wealth. The added value we have are the assets of friends and family that give us the treasure of life.

Nothing we've accomplished as a couple and as a family has been achieved without choice. We had to choose to drive older cars, eat out less, take modest vacations, and forgo designer clothes in the early years. And along the way, the interesting thing is that we found ways to enjoy all these things without spending foolishly or sacrificing generous giving and smart saving.

I believe that a lot more Americans would have less debt if they would trade the temporary for the long term, if they would realize that living the dream means dreaming without debt. The main difference between mainstream America who lives with debt and disaster and mainstream America who lives the rich life is choice: If you choose to follow the 10/10/80 Rule, you are making a choice that will reconnect you with our nation's roots— the value of hard work and purpose in managing money well.

I hear from thousands of families across the country who are answering the call to live the R.I.C.H. life based on the 10/10/80 Rule. These families aren't achieving their goals by learning to manage a multimillion-dollar portfolio. No, that's not their legacy. Rather, these families are doing it by managing their average incomes extraordinarily well. They want to live a legacy of making the world better through their giving, providing for their future by saving, and living within their means by the way they spend. I proudly join this new group of legacy builders.

We may be average investors, but we are above average people—free from debt, actively paying our bills, living in nice homes, driving paid-for cars, funding a retirement, and putting those babies through college. We are the 85 percent that do most of the living and working and dying in this country. So let's show the rest of the world that we can live rich on less and still have more than we ever imagined.

Now that's a legacy worth leaving.

Living Rich for Life Questions

Whose life will be sweeter because you gave?

Whose life will be richer because you saved?

Whose life will be better because you spent wisely?

Acknowledgments

I want to thank my husband, Bob, for catching the vision and running with it and for picking up the slack and carrying it. You faithful leadership makes for a rich life. Thanks go to my precious family: Daniel (Jenn), Philip, Bethany, Jonathan, Joshua, and Missy (Moran, Oriah, and Eden) for their love and support all these years. To those who are related by birth and by marriage, I love you all. There would be no stories, no success, no book without you.

On a professional level, I have to thank Steve Laube, who knew me from the beginning as my first editor, first critic, and final agent. You are my biz mentor and longtime friend; please don't get hit by a bus.

To my publishing friends at WaterBrook: How long I have coveted the idea of being on your team. It's a dream come true! I have to express my deepest gratitude for your enthusiasm and belief in my work. Jeanette Thomason is the greatest editorial director and most tireless cheerleader—you seem to be everywhere at once; I think you are cloned. Stephen Cobb is the fearless leader whose financial background and publishing expertise make my fingers quiver as I type—passing the muster with you is passing indeed! I so value Ken Petersen's incredible expertise and intuition; it was amazing to be able to tap in to that vast reservoir of knowledge. A special thanks goes to Carie Freimuth for your special favor in marketing, as well as Tiffany Lauer and publicist Jane Rohman, and in sales—Lori Addicott, Steve Reed, and Leah Apineru.

Thanks also to the dear friends who are there through thick and thin—you know who you are, and I'm constantly grateful for your support.

Notes

Chapter 1: Little Miss Giver

1. Bill Clinton, *Giving: How Each of Us Can Change the World* (New York: Knopf, 2008), 13.
2. Clinton, *Giving*, 16.
3. "Celebrity Spending Power," *Bankrate.com*, 31 January 2007. www.bankrate.com/ brm/news/Financial_Literacy/movieS_Salary.asp?caret=3c (accessed 1 September 2008).

Chapter 4: Investing for Idiots

1. "Cost and Financial Aid: Princeton University," *MyPlan.com*, 2007. www.myplan .com/education/db/ug/ug_4.php?id=186131.

Chapter 5: Fat Tuesday

1. Liz Pulliam Weston, www.mycreditmatters.biz/youandyourcredit.html.
2. "Issue Brief: Credit Card Fees and Surcharges," *GFOA*, January 2008. www.gfoa .org/downloads/CREDITCARDS.pdf.

Chapter 10: Cruisin' to Vacation Savings

1. Peter Greenberg, "Best Day to Buy Cheap Tix," *Fodor's Travel Wire*, April 2008.

About the Author

Ellie Kay is the best-selling author of *Half-Price Living* and eleven other titles, including *A Tip a Day with Ellie Kay* and *The Debt Diet,* with more than 350,000 books sold. She's a regular television guest on such shows as CNBC's *Power Lunch,* FOX News, and CNN and is a frequently featured family finance expert in numerous magazines and newspapers, including *Family Circle, Women's World,* and *USA Today.* Her financial help columns appear in a dozen periodicals and online. A popular speaker, she's Wal-Mart's official financial help expert and has served as a consumer educator and official spokesperson for Proctor and Gamble, Visa Providian, Master-Card, and more. Ellie and her husband, Bob, are the parents of seven children and live in Palmdale, California.